IT Product Line
Complete Self-Assessment Guide

The guidance in this Self-Assessment is based on IT Product Line best practices and standards in business process architecture, design and quality management. The guidance is also based on the professional judgment of the individual collaborators listed in the Acknowledgments.

Table of Contents

About The Art of Service

The Art of Service, Business Process Architects since 2000, is dedicated to helping stakeholders achieve excellence.

Defining, designing, creating, and implementing a process to solve a stakeholders challenge or meet an objective is the most valuable role… In EVERY group, company, organization and department.

Unless you're talking a one-time, single-use project, there should be a process. Whether that process is managed and implemented by humans, AI, or a combination of the two, it needs to be designed by someone with a complex enough perspective to ask the right questions.

Someone capable of asking the right questions and step back and say, 'What are we really trying to accomplish here? And is there a different way to look at it?'

With The Art of Service's Standard Requirements Self-Assessments, we empower people who can do just that — whether their title is marketer, entrepreneur, manager, salesperson, consultant, Business Process Manager, executive assistant, IT Manager, CIO etc... —they are the people who rule the future. They are people who watch the process as it happens, and ask the right questions to make the process work better.

Contact us when you need any support with this Self-Assessment and any help with templates, blue-prints and examples of standard documents you might need:

http://theartofservice.com
service@theartofservice.com

Acknowledgments

This checklist was developed under the auspices of The Art of Service, chaired by Gerardus Blokdyk.

Representatives from several client companies participated in the preparation of this Self-Assessment.

In addition, we are thankful for the design and printing services provided.

Included Resources - how to access

Included with your purchase of the book is the IT Product Line Self-Assessment Spreadsheet Dashboard which contains all questions and Self-Assessment areas and auto-generates insights, graphs, and project RACI planning - all with examples to get you started right away.

How? Simply send an email to
access@theartofservice.com
with this books' title in the subject to get the IT Product Line Self Assessment Tool right away.

You will receive the following contents with New and Updated specific criteria:

• The latest quick edition of the book in PDF

• The latest complete edition of the book in PDF, which criteria correspond to the criteria in...

• The Self-Assessment Excel Dashboard, and...

• Example pre-filled Self-Assessment Excel Dashboard to get familiar with results generation

• In-depth specific Checklists covering the topic

• Project management checklists and templates to assist with implementation

INCLUDES LIFETIME SELF ASSESSMENT UPDATES

Every self assessment comes with Lifetime Updates and Lifetime Free Updated Books. Lifetime Updates is an industry-first feature which allows you to receive verified self assessment updates, ensuring you always have the most accurate information at your fingertips.

Get it now- you will be glad you did - do it now, before you forget.

Send an email to **access@theartofservice.com** with this books' title in the subject to get the IT Product Line Self Assessment Tool right away.

Your feedback is invaluable to us

If you recently bought this book, we would love to hear from you! You can do this by writing a review on amazon (or the online store where you purchased this book) about your last purchase! As part of our continual service improvement process, we love to hear real client experiences and feedback.

How does it work?

To post a review on Amazon, just log in to your account and click on the Create Your Own Review button (under Customer Reviews) of the relevant product page. You can find examples of product reviews in Amazon. If you purchased from another online store, simply follow their procedures.

What happens when I submit my review?

Once you have submitted your review, send us an email at review@theartofservice.com with the link to your review so we can properly thank you for your feedback.

Purpose of this Self-Assessment

This Self-Assessment has been developed to improve understanding of the requirements and elements of IT Product Line, based on best practices and standards in business process architecture, design and quality management.

It is designed to allow for a rapid Self-Assessment to determine how closely existing management practices and procedures correspond to the elements of the Self-Assessment.

The criteria of requirements and elements of IT Product Line have been rephrased in the format of a Self-Assessment questionnaire, with a seven-criterion scoring system, as explained in this document.

In this format, even with limited background knowledge of IT

Product Line, a manager can quickly review existing operations to determine how they measure up to the standards. This in turn can serve as the starting point of a 'gap analysis' to identify management tools or system elements that might usefully be implemented in the organization to help improve overall performance.

How to use the Self-Assessment

On the following pages are a series of questions to identify to what extent your IT Product Line initiative is complete in comparison to the requirements set in standards.

To facilitate answering the questions, there is a space in front of each question to enter a score on a scale of '1' to '5'.

1 Strongly Disagree

2 Disagree

3 Neutral

4 Agree

5 Strongly Agree

Read the question and rate it with the following in front of mind:

'In my belief,
the answer to this question is clearly defined'.

There are two ways in which you can choose to interpret this statement;
1.   how aware are you that the answer to the question is clearly defined
2.   for more in-depth analysis you can choose to gather

evidence and confirm the answer to the question. This obviously will take more time, most Self-Assessment users opt for the first way to interpret the question and dig deeper later on based on the outcome of the overall Self-Assessment.

A score of '1' would mean that the answer is not clear at all, where a '5' would mean the answer is crystal clear and defined. Leave emtpy when the question is not applicable or you don't want to answer it, you can skip it without affecting your score. Write your score in the space provided.

After you have responded to all the appropriate statements in each section, compute your average score for that section, using the formula provided, and round to the nearest tenth. Then transfer to the corresponding spoke in the IT Product Line Scorecard on the second next page of the Self-Assessment.

Your completed IT Product Line Scorecard will give you a clear presentation of which IT Product Line areas need attention.

IT Product Line
Scorecard Example

Example of how the finalized Scorecard can look like:

IT Product Line
Scorecard

Your Scores:

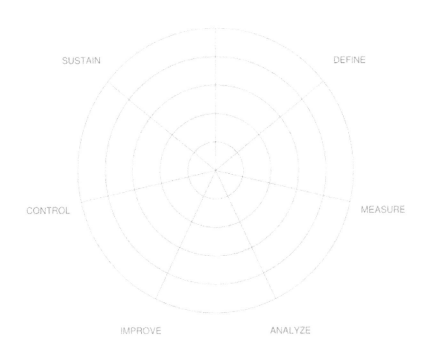

BEGINNING OF THE SELF-ASSESSMENT:

CRITERION #1: RECOGNIZE

INTENT: Be aware of the need for change. Recognize that there is an unfavorable variation, problem or symptom.

In my belief, the answer to this question is clearly defined:

5 Strongly Agree

4 Agree

3 Neutral

2 Disagree

1 Strongly Disagree

1. Does the problem have ethical dimensions?
<--- Score

2. What are the minority interests and what amount of minority interests can be recognized?
<--- Score

3. Are controls defined to recognize and contain problems?

<--- Score

4. What IT product line problem should be solved?
<--- Score

5. What do employees need in the short term?
<--- Score

6. To what extent would your organization benefit from being recognized as a award recipient?
<--- Score

7. Does your organization need more IT product line education?
<--- Score

8. What does IT product line success mean to the stakeholders?
<--- Score

9. Who else hopes to benefit from it?
<--- Score

10. What needs to be done?
<--- Score

11. What IT product line coordination do you need?
<--- Score

12. Why is this needed?
<--- Score

13. How do you assess your IT product line workforce capability and capacity needs, including skills, competencies, and staffing levels?
<--- Score

14. What would happen if IT product line weren't done?
<--- Score

15. How are you going to measure success?
<--- Score

16. What extra resources will you need?
<--- Score

17. What training and capacity building actions are needed to implement proposed reforms?
<--- Score

18. What are the clients issues and concerns?
<--- Score

19. Who should resolve the IT product line issues?
<--- Score

20. How much are sponsors, customers, partners, stakeholders involved in IT product line? In other words, what are the risks, if IT product line does not deliver successfully?
<--- Score

21. Who needs to know about IT product line?
<--- Score

22. What else needs to be measured?
<--- Score

23. Do you know what you need to know about IT product line?
<--- Score

24. When a IT product line manager recognizes a problem, what options are available?
<--- Score

25. Whom do you really need or want to serve?
<--- Score

26. Is it clear when you think of the day ahead of you what activities and tasks you need to complete?
<--- Score

27. Are there recognized IT product line problems?
<--- Score

28. Are you dealing with any of the same issues today as yesterday? What can you do about this?
<--- Score

29. Will a response program recognize when a crisis occurs and provide some level of response?
<--- Score

30. Which needs are not included or involved?
<--- Score

31. Is it needed?
<--- Score

32. Does IT product line create potential expectations in other areas that need to be recognized and considered?
<--- Score

33. Are there IT product line problems defined?
<--- Score

34. Is the quality assurance team identified?

<--- Score

35. Consider your own IT product line project, what types of organizational problems do you think might be causing or affecting your problem, based on the work done so far?

<--- Score

36. What situation(s) led to this IT product line Self Assessment?

<--- Score

37. As a sponsor, customer or management, how important is it to meet goals, objectives?

<--- Score

38. How can auditing be a preventative security measure?

<--- Score

39. What is the problem or issue?

<--- Score

40. What prevents you from making the changes you know will make you a more effective IT product line leader?

<--- Score

41. What needs to stay?

<--- Score

42. Who are your key stakeholders who need to sign off?

<--- Score

43. Have you identified your IT product line key performance indicators?
<--- Score

44. Which issues are too important to ignore?
<--- Score

45. What are your needs in relation to IT product line skills, labor, equipment, and markets?
<--- Score

46. Do you recognize IT product line achievements?
<--- Score

47. What activities does the governance board need to consider?
<--- Score

48. Will new equipment/products be required to facilitate IT product line delivery, for example is new software needed?
<--- Score

49. What is the extent or complexity of the IT product line problem?
<--- Score

50. Are there any specific expectations or concerns about the IT product line team, IT product line itself?
<--- Score

51. Who needs what information?
<--- Score

52. Where is training needed?

<--- Score

53. How do you recognize an objection?
<--- Score

54. What do you need to start doing?
<--- Score

55. Will it solve real problems?
<--- Score

56. Who defines the rules in relation to any given issue?
<--- Score

57. Are employees recognized for desired behaviors?
<--- Score

58. What IT product line capabilities do you need?
<--- Score

59. How do you recognize an IT product line objection?
<--- Score

60. Where do you need to exercise leadership?
<--- Score

61. What creative shifts do you need to take?
<--- Score

62. How does it fit into your organizational needs and tasks?
<--- Score

63. Did you miss any major IT product line issues?
<--- Score

64. What is the smallest subset of the problem you can usefully solve?
<--- Score

65. What are the timeframes required to resolve each of the issues/problems?
<--- Score

66. Are losses recognized in a timely manner?
<--- Score

67. Do you need different information or graphics?
<--- Score

68. What tools and technologies are needed for a custom IT product line project?
<--- Score

69. Are there any revenue recognition issues?
<--- Score

70. Are problem definition and motivation clearly presented?
<--- Score

71. Who needs to know?
<--- Score

72. What are the stakeholder objectives to be achieved with IT product line?
<--- Score

73. What should be considered when identifying

available resources, constraints, and deadlines?
<--- Score

74. Can management personnel recognize the
monetary benefit of IT product line?
<--- Score

75. What is the IT product line problem definition?
What do you need to resolve?
<--- Score

76. What are the expected benefits of IT product line
to the stakeholder?
<--- Score

77. To what extent does each concerned units
management team recognize IT product line as an
effective investment?
<--- Score

78. What is the problem and/or vulnerability?
<--- Score

79. Are employees recognized or rewarded for
performance that demonstrates the highest levels of
integrity?
<--- Score

80. What IT product line events should you attend?
<--- Score

81. Are there regulatory / compliance issues?
<--- Score

82. Who needs budgets?
<--- Score

83. How do you take a forward-looking perspective in identifying IT product line research related to market response and models?
<--- Score

84. Do you need to avoid or amend any IT product line activities?
<--- Score

85. What are the IT product line resources needed?
<--- Score

86. For your IT product line project, identify and describe the business environment, is there more than one layer to the business environment?
<--- Score

87. Think about the people you identified for your IT product line project and the project responsibilities you would assign to them, what kind of training do you think they would need to perform these responsibilities effectively?
<--- Score

88. What problems are you facing and how do you consider IT product line will circumvent those obstacles?
<--- Score

89. Are your goals realistic? Do you need to redefine your problem? Perhaps the problem has changed or maybe you have reached your goal and need to set a new one?
<--- Score

90. How many trainings, in total, are needed?
<--- Score

91. How are training requirements identified?
<--- Score

92. Looking at each person individually – does every one have the qualities which are needed to work in this group?
<--- Score

93. What information do users need?
<--- Score

94. How are the IT product line's objectives aligned to the group's overall stakeholder strategy?
<--- Score

95. Would you recognize a threat from the inside?
<--- Score

96. How do you identify the kinds of information that you will need?
<--- Score

97. Why the need?
<--- Score

Add up total points for this section:
_ _ _ _ _ = Total points for this section

Divided by: _ _ _ _ _ _ (number of statements answered) = _ _ _ _ _ _
Average score for this section

Transfer your score to the IT product

line Index at the beginning of the Self-Assessment.

CRITERION #2: DEFINE:

INTENT: Formulate the stakeholder problem. Define the problem, needs and objectives.

In my belief, the answer to this question is clearly defined:

5 Strongly Agree

4 Agree

3 Neutral

2 Disagree

1 Strongly Disagree

1. Have all basic functions of IT product line been defined?
<--- Score

2. What IT product line services do you require?
<--- Score

3. Is there a clear IT product line case definition?
<--- Score

4. Has the IT product line work been fairly and/or equitably divided and delegated among team members who are qualified and capable to perform the work? Has everyone contributed?
<--- Score

5. Is the improvement team aware of the different versions of a process: what they think it is vs. what it actually is vs. what it should be vs. what it could be?
<--- Score

6. Are all requirements met?
<--- Score

7. Is there a completed SIPOC representation, describing the Suppliers, Inputs, Process, Outputs, and Customers?
<--- Score

8. How can the value of IT product line be defined?
<--- Score

9. Are customer(s) identified and segmented according to their different needs and requirements?
<--- Score

10. How often are the team meetings?
<--- Score

11. Has/have the customer(s) been identified?
<--- Score

12. What knowledge or experience is required?
<--- Score

13. What would be the goal or target for a IT product line's improvement team?
<--- Score

14. Is there regularly 100% attendance at the team meetings? If not, have appointed substitutes attended to preserve cross-functionality and full representation?
<--- Score

15. What is the scope?
<--- Score

16. Is scope creep really all bad news?
<--- Score

17. What IT product line requirements should be gathered?
<--- Score

18. Are different versions of process maps needed to account for the different types of inputs?
<--- Score

19. How will variation in the actual durations of each activity be dealt with to ensure that the expected IT product line results are met?
<--- Score

20. How do you keep key subject matter experts in the loop?
<--- Score

21. Has everyone on the team, including the team leaders, been properly trained?
<--- Score

22. Is the current 'as is' process being followed? If not, what are the discrepancies?
<--- Score

23. Does the team have regular meetings?
<--- Score

24. How do you gather the stories?
<--- Score

25. What gets examined?
<--- Score

26. Has a high-level 'as is' process map been completed, verified and validated?
<--- Score

27. What scope do you want your strategy to cover?
<--- Score

28. What happens if IT product line's scope changes?
<--- Score

29. How do you gather requirements?
<--- Score

30. How do you gather IT product line requirements?
<--- Score

31. Does the scope remain the same?
<--- Score

32. What is the context?
<--- Score

33. Is data collected and displayed to better understand customer(s) critical needs and requirements.
<--- Score

34. Are resources adequate for the scope?
<--- Score

35. How would you define IT product line leadership?
<--- Score

36. What are the requirements for audit information?
<--- Score

37. How does the IT product line manager ensure against scope creep?
<--- Score

38. Will team members perform IT product line work when assigned and in a timely fashion?
<--- Score

39. What specifically is the problem? Where does it occur? When does it occur? What is its extent?
<--- Score

40. Is the scope of IT product line defined?
<--- Score

41. How do you manage unclear IT product line requirements?
<--- Score

42. Will team members regularly document their IT product line work?

<--- Score

43. What is the definition of success?
<--- Score

44. Are required metrics defined, what are they?
<--- Score

45. What are the dynamics of the communication plan?
<--- Score

46. Have the customer needs been translated into specific, measurable requirements? How?
<--- Score

47. Has your scope been defined?
<--- Score

48. How and when will the baselines be defined?
<--- Score

49. Are the IT product line requirements complete?
<--- Score

50. Are there any constraints known that bear on the ability to perform IT product line work? How is the team addressing them?
<--- Score

51. What customer feedback methods were used to solicit their input?
<--- Score

52. Has the direction changed at all during the course of IT product line? If so, when did it change and why?

<--- Score

53. How have you defined all IT product line
requirements first?
<--- Score

54. Is IT product line linked to key stakeholder goals
and objectives?
<--- Score

55. How do you hand over IT product line context?
<--- Score

56. When is the estimated completion date?
<--- Score

57. The political context: who holds power?
<--- Score

58. Do the problem and goal statements meet the
SMART criteria (specific, measurable, attainable,
relevant, and time-bound)?
<--- Score

59. Is the IT product line scope manageable?
<--- Score

60. Is the IT product line scope complete and
appropriately sized?
<--- Score

61. What are the boundaries of the scope? What is in
bounds and what is not? What is the start point? What
is the stop point?
<--- Score

62. How did the IT product line manager receive input to the development of a IT product line improvement plan and the estimated completion dates/times of each activity?
<--- Score

63. Is it clearly defined in and to your organization what you do?
<--- Score

64. Is IT product line required?
<--- Score

65. When are meeting minutes sent out? Who is on the distribution list?
<--- Score

66. Who is gathering IT product line information?
<--- Score

67. Are there different segments of customers?
<--- Score

68. Is there a completed, verified, and validated high-level 'as is' (not 'should be' or 'could be') stakeholder process map?
<--- Score

69. What information do you gather?
<--- Score

70. What are the tasks and definitions?
<--- Score

71. How would you define the culture at your organization, how susceptible is it to IT product

line changes?
<--- Score

72. What is in scope?
<--- Score

73. What are the IT product line use cases?
<--- Score

74. Are roles and responsibilities formally defined?
<--- Score

75. What key stakeholder process output measure(s) does IT product line leverage and how?
<--- Score

76. Have all of the relationships been defined properly?
<--- Score

77. How do you catch IT product line definition inconsistencies?
<--- Score

78. How was the 'as is' process map developed, reviewed, verified and validated?
<--- Score

79. Where can you gather more information?
<--- Score

80. What are the IT product line tasks and definitions?
<--- Score

81. What is in the scope and what is not in scope?

<--- Score

82. What is the scope of the IT product line effort?
<--- Score

83. What critical content must be communicated –
who, what, when, where, and how?
<--- Score

84. How do you think the partners involved in IT
product line would have defined success?
<--- Score

85. Have specific policy objectives been defined?
<--- Score

86. Is IT product line currently on schedule according
to the plan?
<--- Score

87. Has anyone else (internal or external to the group)
attempted to solve this problem or a similar one
before? If so, what knowledge can be leveraged from
these previous efforts?
<--- Score

88. What scope to assess?
<--- Score

89. Are audit criteria, scope, frequency and methods
defined?
<--- Score

90. How do you manage scope?
<--- Score

91. Has a project plan, Gantt chart, or similar been developed/completed?

<--- Score

92. Are accountability and ownership for IT product line clearly defined?

<--- Score

93. How do you manage changes in IT product line requirements?

<--- Score

94. What intelligence can you gather?

<--- Score

95. Has a team charter been developed and communicated?

<--- Score

96. Scope of sensitive information?

<--- Score

97. How will the IT product line team and the group measure complete success of IT product line?

<--- Score

98. What is out-of-scope initially?

<--- Score

99. What are the Roles and Responsibilities for each team member and its leadership? Where is this documented?

<--- Score

100. Do you have a IT product line success story or case study ready to tell and share?

<--- Score

101. What sort of initial information to gather?
<--- Score

102. What is a worst-case scenario for losses?
<--- Score

103. In what way can you redefine the criteria of choice clients have in your category in your favor?
<--- Score

104. Who are the IT product line improvement team members, including Management Leads and Coaches?
<--- Score

105. When is/was the IT product line start date?
<--- Score

106. What are the compelling stakeholder reasons for embarking on IT product line?
<--- Score

107. What are (control) requirements for IT product line Information?
<--- Score

108. Who approved the IT product line scope?
<--- Score

109. Are task requirements clearly defined?
<--- Score

110. If substitutes have been appointed, have they been briefed on the IT product line goals and received

regular communications as to the progress to date?
<--- Score

111. Who is gathering information?
<--- Score

112. What defines best in class?
<--- Score

113. Is there any additional IT product line definition of success?
<--- Score

114. Is there a critical path to deliver IT product line results?
<--- Score

115. Is there a IT product line management charter, including stakeholder case, problem and goal statements, scope, milestones, roles and responsibilities, communication plan?
<--- Score

116. How do you build the right business case?
<--- Score

117. Who defines (or who defined) the rules and roles?
<--- Score

118. What baselines are required to be defined and managed?
<--- Score

119. Is the team adequately staffed with the desired cross-functionality? If not, what additional resources are available to the team?

<--- Score

120. Is the team equipped with available and reliable resources?
<--- Score

121. Is the work to date meeting requirements?
<--- Score

122. Are the IT product line requirements testable?
<--- Score

123. How are consistent IT product line definitions important?
<--- Score

124. Has the improvement team collected the 'voice of the customer' (obtained feedback – qualitative and quantitative)?
<--- Score

125. What is the definition of IT product line excellence?
<--- Score

126. How is the team tracking and documenting its work?
<--- Score

127. What constraints exist that might impact the team?
<--- Score

128. Do you have organizational privacy requirements?
<--- Score

129. What is out of scope?
<--- Score

130. What system do you use for gathering IT product line information?
<--- Score

131. Has a IT product line requirement not been met?
<--- Score

132. What are the core elements of the IT product line business case?
<--- Score

133. What are the record-keeping requirements of IT product line activities?
<--- Score

134. Will a IT product line production readiness review be required?
<--- Score

135. What is the worst case scenario?
<--- Score

136. Do you all define IT product line in the same way?
<--- Score

137. Why are you doing IT product line and what is the scope?
<--- Score

138. What are the rough order estimates on cost savings/opportunities that IT product line brings?
<--- Score

139. What is the scope of the IT product line work?
<--- Score

140. What is the scope of IT product line?
<--- Score

141. What information should you gather?
<--- Score

Add up total points for this section:
_ _ _ _ _ = Total points for this section

Divided by: _ _ _ _ _ _ (number of
statements answered) = _ _ _ _ _ _
Average score for this section

Transfer your score to the IT product
line Index at the beginning of the Self-
Assessment.

CRITERION #3: MEASURE:

INTENT: Gather the correct data.
Measure the current performance and
evolution of the situation.

In my belief, the answer to this
question is clearly defined:

5 Strongly Agree

4 Agree

3 Neutral

2 Disagree

1 Strongly Disagree

1. What users will be impacted?
<--- Score

2. What are the IT product line investment costs?
<--- Score

3. How will your organization measure success?
<--- Score

4. How is progress measured?
<--- Score

5. How will effects be measured?
<--- Score

6. What does losing customers cost your organization?
<--- Score

7. Are you taking your company in the direction of better and revenue or cheaper and cost?
<--- Score

8. Are indirect costs charged to the IT product line program?
<--- Score

9. How can you reduce costs?
<--- Score

10. What tests verify requirements?
<--- Score

11. The approach of traditional IT product line works for detail complexity but is focused on a systematic approach rather than an understanding of the nature of systems themselves, what approach will permit your organization to deal with the kind of unpredictable emergent behaviors that dynamic complexity can introduce?
<--- Score

12. Have you included everything in your IT product line cost models?
<--- Score

13. How can you measure IT product line in a systematic way?
<--- Score

14. What is an unallowable cost?
<--- Score

15. Was a business case (cost/benefit) developed?
<--- Score

16. What is your decision requirements diagram?
<--- Score

17. How do you measure success?
<--- Score

18. Has a cost center been established?
<--- Score

19. How do you control the overall costs of your work processes?
<--- Score

20. Among the IT product line product and service cost to be estimated, which is considered hardest to estimate?
<--- Score

21. Are the measurements objective?
<--- Score

22. Are the units of measure consistent?
<--- Score

23. What are the costs of reform?
<--- Score

24. How do you quantify and qualify impacts?
<--- Score

25. What causes mismanagement?
<--- Score

26. What is the cost of rework?
<--- Score

27. What could cause you to change course?
<--- Score

28. What are the operational costs after IT product line deployment?
<--- Score

29. Do you verify that corrective actions were taken?
<--- Score

30. What are your customers expectations and measures?
<--- Score

31. How do your measurements capture actionable IT product line information for use in exceeding your customers expectations and securing your customers engagement?
<--- Score

32. How sensitive must the IT product line strategy be to cost?
<--- Score

33. What are the IT product line key cost drivers?
<--- Score

34. What measurements are being captured?
<--- Score

35. How are costs allocated?
<--- Score

36. How do you measure lifecycle phases?
<--- Score

37. What could cause delays in the schedule?
<--- Score

38. Do you aggressively reward and promote the people who have the biggest impact on creating excellent IT product line services/products?
<--- Score

39. How do you verify the IT product line requirements quality?
<--- Score

40. What does a Test Case verify?
<--- Score

41. How do you prevent mis-estimating cost?
<--- Score

42. What causes investor action?
<--- Score

43. Is it possible to estimate the impact of unanticipated complexity such as wrong or failed assumptions, feedback, etcetera on proposed reforms?
<--- Score

44. Do you have an issue in getting priority?
<--- Score

45. What is your IT product line quality cost segregation study?
<--- Score

46. Are you able to realize any cost savings?
<--- Score

47. How frequently do you verify your IT product line strategy?
<--- Score

48. What are the costs?
<--- Score

49. What is the total cost related to deploying IT product line, including any consulting or professional services?
<--- Score

50. How do you aggregate measures across priorities?
<--- Score

51. How do you measure efficient delivery of IT product line services?
<--- Score

52. What would it cost to replace your technology?
<--- Score

53. When should you bother with diagrams?
<--- Score

54. Is the cost worth the IT product line effort ?
<--- Score

55. Have design-to-cost goals been established?
<--- Score

56. How do you verify and develop ideas and innovations?
<--- Score

57. What are the strategic priorities for this year?
<--- Score

58. How is the value delivered by IT product line being measured?
<--- Score

59. What does your operating model cost?
<--- Score

60. What does verifying compliance entail?
<--- Score

61. What drives O&M cost?
<--- Score

62. Does a IT product line quantification method exist?
<--- Score

63. What do people want to verify?
<--- Score

64. How do you verify the authenticity of the data and information used?

<--- Score

65. How will measures be used to manage and adapt?
<--- Score

66. What are the current costs of the IT product line process?
<--- Score

67. What are allowable costs?
<--- Score

68. How do you measure variability?
<--- Score

69. What can be used to verify compliance?
<--- Score

70. Does management have the right priorities among projects?
<--- Score

71. Which measures and indicators matter?
<--- Score

72. How to cause the change?
<--- Score

73. Who should receive measurement reports?
<--- Score

74. How do you verify performance?
<--- Score

75. What are you verifying?

<--- Score

76. What is the total fixed cost?
<--- Score

77. How will you measure your IT product line effectiveness?
<--- Score

78. What are hidden IT product line quality costs?
<--- Score

79. What details are required of the IT product line cost structure?
<--- Score

80. Are IT product line vulnerabilities categorized and prioritized?
<--- Score

81. How long to keep data and how to manage retention costs?
<--- Score

82. What are the costs and benefits?
<--- Score

83. Do you have any cost IT product line limitation requirements?
<--- Score

84. What are your key IT product line organizational performance measures, including key short and longer-term financial measures?
<--- Score

85. What would be a real cause for concern?
<--- Score

86. What are your operating costs?
<--- Score

87. How can you manage cost down?
<--- Score

88. What methods are feasible and acceptable to estimate the impact of reforms?
<--- Score

89. Have you made assumptions about the shape of the future, particularly its impact on your customers and competitors?
<--- Score

90. At what cost?
<--- Score

91. How do you stay flexible and focused to recognize larger IT product line results?
<--- Score

92. How much does it cost?
<--- Score

93. Do you effectively measure and reward individual and team performance?
<--- Score

94. Why do the measurements/indicators matter?
<--- Score

95. What are the uncertainties surrounding

estimates of impact?

<--- Score

96. Does the IT product line task fit the client's priorities?

<--- Score

97. What is the IT product line business impact?

<--- Score

98. Who is involved in verifying compliance?

<--- Score

99. Are the IT product line benefits worth its costs?

<--- Score

100. How will costs be allocated?

<--- Score

101. What is the root cause(s) of the problem?

<--- Score

102. Are actual costs in line with budgeted costs?

<--- Score

103. Is a follow-up focused external IT product line review required?

<--- Score

104. Where is the cost?

<--- Score

105. How can a IT product line test verify your ideas or assumptions?

<--- Score

106. Which costs should be taken into account?
<--- Score

107. Which IT product line impacts are significant?
<--- Score

108. What are your primary costs, revenues, assets?
<--- Score

109. Are there any easy-to-implement alternatives to IT product line? Sometimes other solutions are available that do not require the cost implications of a full-blown project?
<--- Score

110. Who pays the cost?
<--- Score

111. What do you measure and why?
<--- Score

112. How is performance measured?
<--- Score

113. What relevant entities could be measured?
<--- Score

114. What are the estimated costs of proposed changes?
<--- Score

115. Why do you expend time and effort to implement measurement, for whom?
<--- Score

116. What is the cause of any IT product line gaps?

<--- Score

117. Where can you go to verify the info?
<--- Score

118. Did you tackle the cause or the symptom?
<--- Score

119. How are you verifying it?
<--- Score

120. Are supply costs steady or fluctuating?
<--- Score

121. How do you verify your resources?
<--- Score

122. What happens if cost savings do not materialize?
<--- Score

123. Do the benefits outweigh the costs?
<--- Score

124. What measurements are possible, practicable and meaningful?
<--- Score

125. What is measured? Why?
<--- Score

126. What evidence is there and what is measured?
<--- Score

127. How frequently do you track IT product line measures?
<--- Score

128. Are there competing IT product line priorities?

<--- Score

129. Will IT product line have an impact on current business continuity, disaster recovery processes and/or infrastructure?

<--- Score

130. How can you reduce the costs of obtaining inputs?

<--- Score

131. How do you focus on what is right -not who is right?

<--- Score

132. What are the costs of delaying IT product line action?

<--- Score

133. Is there an opportunity to verify requirements?

<--- Score

134. How do you verify if IT product line is built right?

<--- Score

135. When are costs are incurred?

<--- Score

136. Are you aware of what could cause a problem?

<--- Score

137. When a disaster occurs, who gets priority?

<--- Score

138. How will success or failure be measured?
<--- Score

139. What disadvantage does this cause for the user?
<--- Score

140. Is the solution cost-effective?
<--- Score

Add up total points for this section:
_ _ _ _ _ = Total points for this section

Divided by: _ _ _ _ _ _ (number of statements answered) = _ _ _ _ _ _
Average score for this section

Transfer your score to the IT product line Index at the beginning of the Self-Assessment.

CRITERION #4: ANALYZE:

INTENT: Analyze causes, assumptions and hypotheses.

In my belief, the answer to this question is clearly defined:

5 Strongly Agree

4 Agree

3 Neutral

2 Disagree

1 Strongly Disagree

1. How many input/output points does it require?
<--- Score

2. Who qualifies to gain access to data?
<--- Score

3. What qualifications do IT product line leaders need?
<--- Score

4. Did any additional data need to be collected?
<--- Score

5. Has data output been validated?
<--- Score

6. What do you need to qualify?
<--- Score

7. What are your key performance measures or indicators and in-process measures for the control and improvement of your IT product line processes?
<--- Score

8. How will the IT product line data be captured?
<--- Score

9. How was the detailed process map generated, verified, and validated?
<--- Score

10. What information qualified as important?
<--- Score

11. Who is involved in the management review process?
<--- Score

12. What data do you need to collect?
<--- Score

13. Is the IT product line process severely broken such that a re-design is necessary?
<--- Score

14. What controls do you have in place to protect data?
<--- Score

15. Was a cause-and-effect diagram used to explore the different types of causes (or sources of variation)?
<--- Score

16. What is the IT product line Driver?
<--- Score

17. What qualifications and skills do you need?
<--- Score

18. Do quality systems drive continuous improvement?
<--- Score

19. Is there a strict change management process?
<--- Score

20. Were any designed experiments used to generate additional insight into the data analysis?
<--- Score

21. What tools were used to generate the list of possible causes?
<--- Score

22. Is pre-qualification of suppliers carried out?
<--- Score

23. How often will data be collected for measures?
<--- Score

24. How do you ensure that the IT product line

opportunity is realistic?
<--- Score

25. Do your contracts/agreements contain data security obligations?
<--- Score

26. Is there any way to speed up the process?
<--- Score

27. Do you understand your management processes today?
<--- Score

28. Do several people in different organizational units assist with the IT product line process?
<--- Score

29. What IT product line data should be managed?
<--- Score

30. Should you invest in industry-recognized qualifications?
<--- Score

31. What, related to, IT product line processes does your organization outsource?
<--- Score

32. How do you use IT product line data and information to support organizational decision making and innovation?
<--- Score

33. What are your current levels and trends in key measures or indicators of IT product line product

and process performance that are important to and directly serve your customers? How do these results compare with the performance of your competitors and other organizations with similar offerings?
<--- Score

34. How will the data be checked for quality?
<--- Score

35. What is the Value Stream Mapping?
<--- Score

36. Is the required IT product line data gathered?
<--- Score

37. Have the problem and goal statements been updated to reflect the additional knowledge gained from the analyze phase?
<--- Score

38. What were the financial benefits resulting from any 'ground fruit or low-hanging fruit' (quick fixes)?
<--- Score

39. Has an output goal been set?
<--- Score

40. What IT product line data should be collected?
<--- Score

41. Is the suppliers process defined and controlled?
<--- Score

42. Is the final output clearly identified?
<--- Score

43. Which IT product line data should be retained?
<--- Score

44. What kind of crime could a potential new hire have committed that would not only not disqualify him/her from being hired by your organization, but would actually indicate that he/she might be a particularly good fit?
<--- Score

45. How can risk management be tied procedurally to process elements?
<--- Score

46. Is data and process analysis, root cause analysis and quantifying the gap/opportunity in place?
<--- Score

47. How has the IT product line data been gathered?
<--- Score

48. Have you defined which data is gathered how?
<--- Score

49. Do you have the authority to produce the output?
<--- Score

50. Where is the data coming from to measure compliance?
<--- Score

51. Do your employees have the opportunity to do what they do best everyday?
<--- Score

52. Who gets your output?
<--- Score

53. What IT product line data do you gather or use now?
<--- Score

54. What qualifies as competition?
<--- Score

55. What types of data do your IT product line indicators require?
<--- Score

56. Who is involved with workflow mapping?
<--- Score

57. How do you measure the operational performance of your key work systems and processes, including productivity, cycle time, and other appropriate measures of process effectiveness, efficiency, and innovation?
<--- Score

58. Think about some of the processes you undertake within your organization, which do you own?
<--- Score

59. What IT product line metrics are outputs of the process?
<--- Score

60. Are all staff in core IT product line subjects Highly Qualified?
<--- Score

61. How is the data gathered?

<--- Score

62. What data is gathered?

<--- Score

63. What process improvements will be needed?

<--- Score

64. How do you identify specific IT product line investment opportunities and emerging trends?

<--- Score

65. What resources go in to get the desired output?

<--- Score

66. Think about the functions involved in your IT product line project, what processes flow from these functions?

<--- Score

67. Who will gather what data?

<--- Score

68. What are evaluation criteria for the output?

<--- Score

69. What methods do you use to gather IT product line data?

<--- Score

70. Was a detailed process map created to amplify critical steps of the 'as is' stakeholder process?

<--- Score

71. What IT product line data will be collected?
<--- Score

72. What is the oversight process?
<--- Score

73. What are your outputs?
<--- Score

74. How does the organization define, manage, and improve its IT product line processes?
<--- Score

75. What does the data say about the performance of the stakeholder process?
<--- Score

76. What is the cost of poor quality as supported by the team's analysis?
<--- Score

77. How do you promote understanding that opportunity for improvement is not criticism of the status quo, or the people who created the status quo?
<--- Score

78. What tools were used to narrow the list of possible causes?
<--- Score

79. What were the crucial 'moments of truth' on the process map?
<--- Score

80. What conclusions were drawn from the team's data collection and analysis? How did the team reach

these conclusions?
<--- Score

81. What training and qualifications will you need?
<--- Score

82. What are the best opportunities for value improvement?
<--- Score

83. Do you, as a leader, bounce back quickly from setbacks?
<--- Score

84. Is the performance gap determined?
<--- Score

85. What are the personnel training and qualifications required?
<--- Score

86. What will drive IT product line change?
<--- Score

87. What did the team gain from developing a sub-process map?
<--- Score

88. An organizationally feasible system request is one that considers the mission, goals and objectives of the organization, key questions are: is the IT product line solution request practical and will it solve a problem or take advantage of an opportunity to achieve company goals?
<--- Score

89. How do your work systems and key work processes relate to and capitalize on your core competencies?
<--- Score

90. Who will facilitate the team and process?
<--- Score

91. Have any additional benefits been identified that will result from closing all or most of the gaps?
<--- Score

92. Do staff qualifications match your project?
<--- Score

93. What is your organizations process which leads to recognition of value generation?
<--- Score

94. What is the complexity of the output produced?
<--- Score

95. How do you define collaboration and team output?
<--- Score

96. How is the way you as the leader think and process information affecting your organizational culture?
<--- Score

97. Are IT product line changes recognized early enough to be approved through the regular process?
<--- Score

98. Is the gap/opportunity displayed and

communicated in financial terms?
<--- Score

99. How is the IT product line Value Stream Mapping managed?
<--- Score

100. What are the IT product line design outputs?
<--- Score

101. What are the IT product line business drivers?
<--- Score

102. What other jobs or tasks affect the performance of the steps in the IT product line process?
<--- Score

103. Identify an operational issue in your organization, for example, could a particular task be done more quickly or more efficiently by IT product line?
<--- Score

104. What qualifications are necessary?
<--- Score

105. Are you missing IT product line opportunities?
<--- Score

106. Who owns what data?
<--- Score

107. Record-keeping requirements flow from the records needed as inputs, outputs, controls and for transformation of a IT product line process, are the records needed as inputs to the IT product line process available?

<--- Score

108. Do your leaders quickly bounce back from setbacks?
<--- Score

109. How do mission and objectives affect the IT product line processes of your organization?
<--- Score

110. Are your outputs consistent?
<--- Score

111. What process should you select for improvement?
<--- Score

112. What are your best practices for minimizing IT product line project risk, while demonstrating incremental value and quick wins throughout the IT product line project lifecycle?
<--- Score

113. What are the necessary qualifications?
<--- Score

114. Is there an established change management process?
<--- Score

115. What are the revised rough estimates of the financial savings/opportunity for IT product line improvements?
<--- Score

116. How do you implement and manage your

work processes to ensure that they meet design requirements?
<--- Score

117. Were Pareto charts (or similar) used to portray the 'heavy hitters' (or key sources of variation)?
<--- Score

118. Are all team members qualified for all tasks?
<--- Score

119. What internal processes need improvement?
<--- Score

120. What quality tools were used to get through the analyze phase?
<--- Score

121. What are your current levels and trends in key IT product line measures or indicators of product and process performance that are important to and directly serve your customers?
<--- Score

122. What is your organizations system for selecting qualified vendors?
<--- Score

123. Did any value-added analysis or 'lean thinking' take place to identify some of the gaps shown on the 'as is' process map?
<--- Score

124. A compounding model resolution with available relevant data can often provide insight towards a solution methodology; which IT product line models,

tools and techniques are necessary?
<--- Score

125. How is data used for program management and improvement?
<--- Score

126. Can you add value to the current IT product line decision-making process (largely qualitative) by incorporating uncertainty modeling (more quantitative)?
<--- Score

127. Where is IT product line data gathered?
<--- Score

128. What qualifications are needed?
<--- Score

129. How are outputs preserved and protected?
<--- Score

130. What are the disruptive IT product line technologies that enable your organization to radically change your business processes?
<--- Score

131. Were there any improvement opportunities identified from the process analysis?
<--- Score

Add up total points for this section:
_ _ _ _ _ = Total points for this section

Divided by: _ _ _ _ _ _ (number of statements answered) = _ _ _ _ _ _

Average score for this section

Transfer your score to the IT product
line Index at the beginning of the Self-
Assessment.

CRITERION #5: IMPROVE:

INTENT: Develop a practical solution. Innovate, establish and test the solution and to measure the results.

In my belief, the answer to this question is clearly defined:

5 Strongly Agree

4 Agree

3 Neutral

2 Disagree

1 Strongly Disagree

1. Are the most efficient solutions problem-specific?
<--- Score

2. What are the affordable IT product line risks?
<--- Score

3. Who are the people involved in developing and implementing IT product line?
<--- Score

4. Can you integrate quality management and risk management?
<--- Score

5. How can the phases of IT product line development be identified?
<--- Score

6. What error proofing will be done to address some of the discrepancies observed in the 'as is' process?
<--- Score

7. Who controls the risk?
<--- Score

8. How are IT product line risks managed?
<--- Score

9. Do you have the optimal project management team structure?
<--- Score

10. In the past few months, what is the smallest change you have made that has had the biggest positive result? What was it about that small change that produced the large return?
<--- Score

11. Do vendor agreements bring new compliance risk ?
<--- Score

12. How is knowledge sharing about risk management improved?
<--- Score

13. Explorations of the frontiers of IT product line will help you build influence, improve IT product line, optimize decision making, and sustain change, what is your approach?
<--- Score

14. How do you define the solutions' scope?
<--- Score

15. Are risk triggers captured?
<--- Score

16. What to do with the results or outcomes of measurements?
<--- Score

17. Is the IT product line documentation thorough?
<--- Score

18. Which IT product line solution is appropriate?
<--- Score

19. How will you know that a change is an improvement?
<--- Score

20. How can skill-level changes improve IT product line?
<--- Score

21. What IT product line improvements can be made?
<--- Score

22. How do you manage and improve your IT product line work systems to deliver customer value and

achieve organizational success and sustainability?
<--- Score

23. How do you link measurement and risk?
<--- Score

24. How will you measure the results?
<--- Score

25. What resources are required for the improvement efforts?
<--- Score

26. Can the solution be designed and implemented within an acceptable time period?
<--- Score

27. To what extent does management recognize IT product line as a tool to increase the results?
<--- Score

28. What attendant changes will need to be made to ensure that the solution is successful?
<--- Score

29. Which of the recognised risks out of all risks can be most likely transferred?
<--- Score

30. How risky is your organization?
<--- Score

31. How significant is the improvement in the eyes of the end user?
<--- Score

32. What is the IT product line's sustainability risk?
<--- Score

33. What tools were used to evaluate the potential solutions?
<--- Score

34. Are risk management tasks balanced centrally and locally?
<--- Score

35. What is the team's contingency plan for potential problems occurring in implementation?
<--- Score

36. What assumptions are made about the solution and approach?
<--- Score

37. How do you measure risk?
<--- Score

38. What are the concrete IT product line results?
<--- Score

39. How can you better manage risk?
<--- Score

40. Who will be responsible for making the decisions to include or exclude requested changes once IT product line is underway?
<--- Score

41. What are the expected IT product line results?
<--- Score

42. Were any criteria developed to assist the team in testing and evaluating potential solutions?

<--- Score

43. What criteria will you use to assess your IT product line risks?

<--- Score

44. What tools were most useful during the improve phase?

<--- Score

45. How do you improve IT product line service perception, and satisfaction?

<--- Score

46. Have you achieved IT product line improvements?

<--- Score

47. Is the measure of success for IT product line understandable to a variety of people?

<--- Score

48. Do those selected for the IT product line team have a good general understanding of what IT product line is all about?

<--- Score

49. How will you know that you have improved?

<--- Score

50. What is IT product line's impact on utilizing the best solution(s)?

<--- Score

51. How will you recognize and celebrate results?
<--- Score

52. How do you improve your likelihood of success ?
<--- Score

53. Is there a cost/benefit analysis of optimal solution(s)?
<--- Score

54. Do you combine technical expertise with business knowledge and IT product line Key topics include lifecycles, development approaches, requirements and how to make a business case?
<--- Score

55. How can you improve performance?
<--- Score

56. Are the key business and technology risks being managed?
<--- Score

57. How do you manage IT product line risk?
<--- Score

58. Who should make the IT product line decisions?
<--- Score

59. Does the goal represent a desired result that can be measured?
<--- Score

60. What lessons, if any, from a pilot were incorporated into the design of the full-scale solution?
<--- Score

61. What went well, what should change, what can improve?
<--- Score

62. What strategies for IT product line improvement are successful?
<--- Score

63. Who manages supplier risk management in your organization?
<--- Score

64. How do you deal with IT product line risk?
<--- Score

65. What tools were used to tap into the creativity and encourage 'outside the box' thinking?
<--- Score

66. Who are the key stakeholders for the IT product line evaluation?
<--- Score

67. What do you want to improve?
<--- Score

68. Is there a high likelihood that any recommendations will achieve their intended results?
<--- Score

69. What should a proof of concept or pilot accomplish?
<--- Score

70. Is risk periodically assessed?

<--- Score

71. Are events managed to resolution?
<--- Score

72. Is the optimal solution selected based on testing and analysis?
<--- Score

73. When you map the key players in your own work and the types/domains of relationships with them, which relationships do you find easy and which challenging, and why?
<--- Score

74. Who do you report IT product line results to?
<--- Score

75. What are your current levels and trends in key measures or indicators of workforce and leader development?
<--- Score

76. Who will be responsible for documenting the IT product line requirements in detail?
<--- Score

77. Are you assessing IT product line and risk?
<--- Score

78. Is the IT product line risk managed?
<--- Score

79. Are procedures documented for managing IT product line risks?
<--- Score

80. How is continuous improvement applied to risk management?
<--- Score

81. What does the 'should be' process map/design look like?
<--- Score

82. What are the IT product line security risks?
<--- Score

83. What is the magnitude of the improvements?
<--- Score

84. Are the risks fully understood, reasonable and manageable?
<--- Score

85. What improvements have been achieved?
<--- Score

86. How do you improve productivity?
<--- Score

87. How do you measure progress and evaluate training effectiveness?
<--- Score

88. How does your organization evaluate strategic IT product line success?
<--- Score

89. Can you identify any significant risks or exposures to IT product line third- parties (vendors, service providers, alliance partners etc) that concern you?

<--- Score

90. Is there any other IT product line solution?
<--- Score

91. Is there a small-scale pilot for proposed improvement(s)? What conclusions were drawn from the outcomes of a pilot?
<--- Score

92. Where do the IT product line decisions reside?
<--- Score

93. Have you identified breakpoints and/or risk tolerances that will trigger broad consideration of a potential need for intervention or modification of strategy?
<--- Score

94. How will you know when its improved?
<--- Score

95. What tools do you use once you have decided on a IT product line strategy and more importantly how do you choose?
<--- Score

96. What actually has to improve and by how much?
<--- Score

97. IT product line risk decisions: whose call Is It?
<--- Score

98. If you could go back in time five years, what decision would you make differently? What is

your best guess as to what decision you're making today you might regret five years from now?
<--- Score

99. What is the risk?
<--- Score

100. Who makes the IT product line decisions in your organization?
<--- Score

101. What current systems have to be understood and/or changed?
<--- Score

102. What are the implications of the one critical IT product line decision 10 minutes, 10 months, and 10 years from now?
<--- Score

103. Do you need to do a usability evaluation?
<--- Score

104. How scalable is your IT product line solution?
<--- Score

105. What risks do you need to manage?
<--- Score

106. How do you go about comparing IT product line approaches/solutions?
<--- Score

107. Who will be using the results of the measurement activities?
<--- Score

108. Who manages IT product line risk?
<--- Score

109. How does the team improve its work?
<--- Score

110. Do you cover the five essential competencies:
Communication, Collaboration,Innovation,
Adaptability, and Leadership that improve an
organizations ability to leverage the new IT product
line in a volatile global economy?
<--- Score

**111. What practices helps your organization to
develop its capacity to recognize patterns?**
<--- Score

112. Why improve in the first place?
<--- Score

**113. Risk factors: what are the characteristics of IT
product line that make it risky?**
<--- Score

114. How do you keep improving IT product line?
<--- Score

115. What communications are necessary to support
the implementation of the solution?
<--- Score

116. Was a IT product line charter developed?
<--- Score

117. What were the criteria for evaluating a IT product

line pilot?
<--- Score

118. Is supporting IT product line documentation required?
<--- Score

119. How are policy decisions made and where?
<--- Score

120. Will the controls trigger any other risks?
<--- Score

121. Risk Identification: What are the possible risk events your organization faces in relation to IT product line?
<--- Score

122. Was a pilot designed for the proposed solution(s)?
<--- Score

123. Who controls key decisions that will be made?
<--- Score

124. How do you mitigate IT product line risk?
<--- Score

125. What were the underlying assumptions on the cost-benefit analysis?
<--- Score

126. How do you measure improved IT product line service perception, and satisfaction?
<--- Score

127. Are decisions made in a timely manner?
<--- Score

128. What can you do to improve?
<--- Score

129. Is any IT product line documentation required?
<--- Score

130. For estimation problems, how do you develop an estimation statement?
<--- Score

131. Is the IT product line solution sustainable?
<--- Score

132. What is the implementation plan?
<--- Score

133. Where do you need IT product line improvement?
<--- Score

134. Does a good decision guarantee a good outcome?
<--- Score

135. How can you improve IT product line?
<--- Score

136. How do you decide how much to remunerate an employee?
<--- Score

137. What alternative responses are available to manage risk?

<--- Score

138. At what point will vulnerability assessments be performed once IT product line is put into production (e.g., ongoing Risk Management after implementation)?
<--- Score

139. How do the IT product line results compare with the performance of your competitors and other organizations with similar offerings?
<--- Score

Add up total points for this section:
_ _ _ _ _ = Total points for this section

Divided by: _ _ _ _ _ _ (number of statements answered) = _ _ _ _ _ _
Average score for this section

Transfer your score to the IT product line Index at the beginning of the Self-Assessment.

CRITERION #6: CONTROL:

In my belief, the answer to this
question is clearly defined:

5 Strongly Agree

4 Agree

3 Neutral

2 Disagree

1 Strongly Disagree

1. In the case of a IT product line project, the criteria
for the audit derive from implementation objectives,
an audit of a IT product line project involves
assessing whether the recommendations outlined
for implementation have been met, can you track
that any IT product line project is implemented as
planned, and is it working?
<--- Score

2. Is new knowledge gained imbedded in the response plan?
<--- Score

3. What can you control?
<--- Score

4. How will input, process, and output variables be checked to detect for sub-optimal conditions?
<--- Score

5. Are the planned controls in place?
<--- Score

6. What are you attempting to measure/monitor?
<--- Score

7. How will the process owner verify improvement in present and future sigma levels, process capabilities?
<--- Score

8. What do you measure to verify effectiveness gains?
<--- Score

9. How widespread is its use?
<--- Score

10. Against what alternative is success being measured?
<--- Score

11. Is there an action plan in case of emergencies?
<--- Score

12. How will you measure your QA plan's

effectiveness?
<--- Score

13. Has the improved process and its steps been standardized?
<--- Score

14. How will IT product line decisions be made and monitored?
<--- Score

15. You may have created your quality measures at a time when you lacked resources, technology wasn't up to the required standard, or low service levels were the industry norm. Have those circumstances changed?
<--- Score

16. What should you measure to verify efficiency gains?
<--- Score

17. Are new process steps, standards, and documentation ingrained into normal operations?
<--- Score

18. What key inputs and outputs are being measured on an ongoing basis?
<--- Score

19. Is reporting being used or needed?
<--- Score

20. What is the best design framework for IT product line organization now that, in a post industrial-age if the top-down, command and control model is no

longer relevant?
<--- Score

21. Will existing staff require re-training, for example, to learn new business processes?
<--- Score

22. How do senior leaders actions reflect a commitment to the organizations IT product line values?
<--- Score

23. Are controls in place and consistently applied?
<--- Score

24. Does job training on the documented procedures need to be part of the process team's education and training?
<--- Score

25. How do you encourage people to take control and responsibility?
<--- Score

26. Is there a transfer of ownership and knowledge to process owner and process team tasked with the responsibilities.
<--- Score

27. What IT product line standards are applicable?
<--- Score

28. What other systems, operations, processes, and infrastructures (hiring practices, staffing, training, incentives/rewards, metrics/dashboards/scorecards, etc.) need updates, additions, changes, or deletions

in order to facilitate knowledge transfer and improvements?

<--- Score

29. How do you plan for the cost of succession?

<--- Score

30. Are documented procedures clear and easy to follow for the operators?

<--- Score

31. What do you stand for--and what are you against?

<--- Score

32. Are pertinent alerts monitored, analyzed and distributed to appropriate personnel?

<--- Score

33. Who sets the IT product line standards?

<--- Score

34. How do you spread information?

<--- Score

35. What is the control/monitoring plan?

<--- Score

36. Will any special training be provided for results interpretation?

<--- Score

37. Are you measuring, monitoring and predicting IT product line activities to optimize operations and profitability, and enhancing outcomes?

<--- Score

38. What are the critical parameters to watch?
<--- Score

39. How do you plan on providing proper recognition and disclosure of supporting companies?
<--- Score

40. What are the key elements of your IT product line performance improvement system, including your evaluation, organizational learning, and innovation processes?
<--- Score

41. What are customers monitoring?
<--- Score

42. Is there a recommended audit plan for routine surveillance inspections of IT product line's gains?
<--- Score

43. Is a response plan established and deployed?
<--- Score

44. What are the known security controls?
<--- Score

45. Does a troubleshooting guide exist or is it needed?
<--- Score

46. Act/Adjust: What Do you Need to Do Differently?
<--- Score

47. Who controls critical resources?
<--- Score

48. How is change control managed?

<--- Score

49. Do the viable solutions scale to future needs?
<--- Score

50. Is there a documented and implemented monitoring plan?
<--- Score

51. Who has control over resources?
<--- Score

52. Do you monitor the IT product line decisions made and fine tune them as they evolve?
<--- Score

53. What is your theory of human motivation, and how does your compensation plan fit with that view?
<--- Score

54. Does the response plan contain a definite closed loop continual improvement scheme (e.g., plan-do-check-act)?
<--- Score

55. Will your goals reflect your program budget?
<--- Score

56. Will the team be available to assist members in planning investigations?
<--- Score

57. Is there a control plan in place for sustaining improvements (short and long-term)?
<--- Score

58. Are the planned controls working?
<--- Score

59. How might the group capture best practices and lessons learned so as to leverage improvements?
<--- Score

60. How likely is the current IT product line plan to come in on schedule or on budget?
<--- Score

61. What other areas of the group might benefit from the IT product line team's improvements, knowledge, and learning?
<--- Score

62. How can you best use all of your knowledge repositories to enhance learning and sharing?
<--- Score

63. How do controls support value?
<--- Score

64. What should the next improvement project be that is related to IT product line?
<--- Score

65. Does the IT product line performance meet the customer's requirements?
<--- Score

66. Who is the IT product line process owner?
<--- Score

67. How do your controls stack up?
<--- Score

68. Who is going to spread your message?
<--- Score

69. Can support from partners be adjusted?
<--- Score

70. Is the IT product line test/monitoring cost justified?
<--- Score

71. Are the IT product line standards challenging?
<--- Score

72. What is your plan to assess your security risks?
<--- Score

73. What are your results for key measures or indicators of the accomplishment of your IT product line strategy and action plans, including building and strengthening core competencies?
<--- Score

74. What quality tools were useful in the control phase?
<--- Score

75. Is knowledge gained on process shared and institutionalized?
<--- Score

76. Can you adapt and adjust to changing IT product line situations?
<--- Score

77. What are the performance and scale of the IT

product line tools?
<--- Score

78. Is there a IT product line Communication plan covering who needs to get what information when?
<--- Score

79. Who will be in control?
<--- Score

80. Is there a standardized process?
<--- Score

81. Are there documented procedures?
<--- Score

82. What is the recommended frequency of auditing?
<--- Score

83. How will the day-to-day responsibilities for monitoring and continual improvement be transferred from the improvement team to the process owner?
<--- Score

84. Is a response plan in place for when the input, process, or output measures indicate an 'out-of-control' condition?
<--- Score

85. Do you monitor the effectiveness of your IT product line activities?
<--- Score

86. Does IT product line appropriately measure and monitor risk?

<--- Score

87. What adjustments to the strategies are needed?
<--- Score

88. How will the process owner and team be able to hold the gains?
<--- Score

89. How do you establish and deploy modified action plans if circumstances require a shift in plans and rapid execution of new plans?
<--- Score

90. Where do ideas that reach policy makers and planners as proposals for IT product line strengthening and reform actually originate?
<--- Score

91. Implementation Planning: is a pilot needed to test the changes before a full roll out occurs?
<--- Score

92. Are operating procedures consistent?
<--- Score

93. Has the IT product line value of standards been quantified?
<--- Score

94. How do you select, collect, align, and integrate IT product line data and information for tracking daily operations and overall organizational performance, including progress relative to strategic objectives and action plans?

<--- Score

95. Do the IT product line decisions you make today help people and the planet tomorrow?
<--- Score

96. What do your reports reflect?
<--- Score

97. Is there documentation that will support the successful operation of the improvement?
<--- Score

98. Have new or revised work instructions resulted?
<--- Score

99. How will new or emerging customer needs/ requirements be checked/communicated to orient the process toward meeting the new specifications and continually reducing variation?
<--- Score

100. What is the standard for acceptable IT product line performance?
<--- Score

101. Are suggested corrective/restorative actions indicated on the response plan for known causes to problems that might surface?
<--- Score

102. How will report readings be checked to effectively monitor performance?
<--- Score

Add up total points for this section:

_____ = Total points for this section

Divided by: _____ (number of
statements answered) = _____
Average score for this section

Transfer your score to the IT product
line Index at the beginning of the Self-
Assessment.

CRITERION #7: SUSTAIN:

INTENT: Retain the benefits.

In my belief, the answer to this question is clearly defined:

5 Strongly Agree

4 Agree

3 Neutral

2 Disagree

1 Strongly Disagree

1. What is a feasible sequencing of reform initiatives over time?
<--- Score

2. What are your personal philosophies regarding IT product line and how do they influence your work?
<--- Score

3. How long will it take to change?
<--- Score

4. How do you accomplish your long range IT product line goals?

<--- Score

5. What trouble can you get into?

<--- Score

6. What are the barriers to increased IT product line production?

<--- Score

7. How do you foster innovation?

<--- Score

8. What have been your experiences in defining long range IT product line goals?

<--- Score

9. Do you see more potential in people than they do in themselves?

<--- Score

10. What is an unauthorized commitment?

<--- Score

11. What are the usability implications of IT product line actions?

<--- Score

12. What knowledge, skills and characteristics mark a good IT product line project manager?

<--- Score

13. Can you do all this work?

<--- Score

14. Who, on the executive team or the board, has spoken to a customer recently?
<--- Score

15. Who are the key stakeholders?
<--- Score

16. How do you set IT product line stretch targets and how do you get people to not only participate in setting these stretch targets but also that they strive to achieve these?
<--- Score

17. Do you think IT product line accomplishes the goals you expect it to accomplish?
<--- Score

18. Are you using a design thinking approach and integrating Innovation, IT product line Experience, and Brand Value?
<--- Score

19. How do you listen to customers to obtain actionable information?
<--- Score

20. What does your signature ensure?
<--- Score

21. Who have you, as a company, historically been when you've been at your best?
<--- Score

22. Do you have the right capabilities and capacities?
<--- Score

23. How do you make it meaningful in connecting IT product line with what users do day-to-day?
<--- Score

24. How will you insure seamless interoperability of IT product line moving forward?
<--- Score

25. What are current IT product line paradigms?
<--- Score

26. Who is on the team?
<--- Score

27. Why will customers want to buy your organizations products/services?
<--- Score

28. What was the last experiment you ran?
<--- Score

29. How do you govern and fulfill your societal responsibilities?
<--- Score

30. When information truly is ubiquitous, when reach and connectivity are completely global, when computing resources are infinite, and when a whole new set of impossibilities are not only possible, but happening, what will that do to your business?
<--- Score

31. How is implementation research currently incorporated into each of your goals?
<--- Score

32. Operational - will it work?
<--- Score

33. What is the funding source for this project?
<--- Score

34. Do you feel that more should be done in the IT product line area?
<--- Score

35. What is the overall business strategy?
<--- Score

36. What are the essentials of internal IT product line management?
<--- Score

37. Whom among your colleagues do you trust, and for what?
<--- Score

38. How do you ensure that implementations of IT product line products are done in a way that ensures safety?
<--- Score

39. How can you become the company that would put you out of business?
<--- Score

40. Will there be any necessary staff changes (redundancies or new hires)?
<--- Score

41. Who is responsible for ensuring appropriate

resources (time, people and money) are allocated to IT product line?
<--- Score

42. Is there a work around that you can use?
<--- Score

43. Are you relevant? Will you be relevant five years from now? Ten?
<--- Score

44. Is IT product line dependent on the successful delivery of a current project?
<--- Score

45. Political -is anyone trying to undermine this project?
<--- Score

46. How important is IT product line to the user organizations mission?
<--- Score

47. Are you maintaining a past–present–future perspective throughout the IT product line discussion?
<--- Score

48. Ask yourself: how would you do this work if you only had one staff member to do it?
<--- Score

49. What are your most important goals for the strategic IT product line objectives?
<--- Score

50. What is the purpose of IT product line in relation to the mission?

<--- Score

51. What management system can you use to leverage the IT product line experience, ideas, and concerns of the people closest to the work to be done?

<--- Score

52. Instead of going to current contacts for new ideas, what if you reconnected with dormant contacts--the people you used to know? If you were going reactivate a dormant tie, who would it be?

<--- Score

53. What should you stop doing?

<--- Score

54. Do IT product line rules make a reasonable demand on a users capabilities?

<--- Score

55. What is your question? Why?

<--- Score

56. Are assumptions made in IT product line stated explicitly?

<--- Score

57. Why not do IT product line?

<--- Score

58. What role does communication play in the success or failure of a IT product line project?

<--- Score

59. If you find that you havent accomplished one of the goals for one of the steps of the IT product line strategy, what will you do to fix it?
<--- Score

60. What are the potential basics of IT product line fraud?
<--- Score

61. What are strategies for increasing support and reducing opposition?
<--- Score

62. Is it economical; do you have the time and money?
<--- Score

63. If you do not follow, then how to lead?
<--- Score

64. Is IT product line realistic, or are you setting yourself up for failure?
<--- Score

65. What could happen if you do not do it?
<--- Score

66. Who are your customers?
<--- Score

67. What is the kind of project structure that would be appropriate for your IT product line project, should it be formal and complex, or can it be less formal and relatively simple?
<--- Score

68. What would you recommend your friend do if he/she were facing this dilemma?

<--- Score

69. What must you excel at?

<--- Score

70. How do you transition from the baseline to the target?

<--- Score

71. Is maximizing IT product line protection the same as minimizing IT product line loss?

<--- Score

72. What new services of functionality will be implemented next with IT product line ?

<--- Score

73. Can you maintain your growth without detracting from the factors that have contributed to your success?

<--- Score

74. Did your employees make progress today?

<--- Score

75. Why should you adopt a IT product line framework?

<--- Score

76. How do you manage IT product line Knowledge Management (KM)?

<--- Score

77. What IT product line skills are most important?
<--- Score

78. Why should people listen to you?
<--- Score

79. Would you rather sell to knowledgeable and informed customers or to uninformed customers?
<--- Score

80. What happens when a new employee joins the organization?
<--- Score

81. How are you doing compared to your industry?
<--- Score

82. Who do you think the world wants your organization to be?
<--- Score

83. If you had to leave your organization for a year and the only communication you could have with employees/colleagues was a single paragraph, what would you write?
<--- Score

84. What are the key enablers to make this IT product line move?
<--- Score

85. What IT product line modifications can you make work for you?
<--- Score

86. How do customers see your organization?

<--- Score

87. What goals did you miss?
<--- Score

88. Where can you break convention?
<--- Score

89. What is the range of capabilities?
<--- Score

90. In a project to restructure IT product line outcomes, which stakeholders would you involve?
<--- Score

91. Who are four people whose careers you have enhanced?
<--- Score

92. Which IT product line goals are the most important?
<--- Score

93. Who will determine interim and final deadlines?
<--- Score

94. What is the recommended frequency of auditing?
<--- Score

95. How will you ensure you get what you expected?
<--- Score

96. How do you know if you are successful?
<--- Score

97. Is there any reason to believe the opposite of my current belief?
<--- Score

98. How do you keep records, of what?
<--- Score

99. Why is it important to have senior management support for a IT product line project?
<--- Score

100. What would have to be true for the option on the table to be the best possible choice?
<--- Score

101. How do you create buy-in?
<--- Score

102. What relationships among IT product line trends do you perceive?
<--- Score

103. Which functions and people interact with the supplier and or customer?
<--- Score

104. Can the schedule be done in the given time?
<--- Score

105. What is the estimated value of the project?
<--- Score

106. How can you incorporate support to ensure safe and effective use of IT product line into the services that you provide?
<--- Score

107. Are you changing as fast as the world around you?
<--- Score

108. Is your basic point _____ or _____?
<--- Score

109. What you are going to do to affect the numbers?
<--- Score

110. Who will provide the final approval of IT product line deliverables?
<--- Score

111. Who is responsible for errors?
<--- Score

112. What projects are going on in the organization today, and what resources are those projects using from the resource pools?
<--- Score

113. What is the overall talent health of your organization as a whole at senior levels, and for each organization reporting to a member of the Senior Leadership Team?
<--- Score

114. Who will be responsible for deciding whether IT product line goes ahead or not after the initial investigations?
<--- Score

115. Do you have enough freaky customers in your portfolio pushing you to the limit day in and day

out?
<--- Score

116. What is effective IT product line?
<--- Score

117. What are the long-term IT product line goals?
<--- Score

118. What is the craziest thing you can do?
<--- Score

119. How do you provide a safe environment -physically and emotionally?
<--- Score

120. Will it be accepted by users?
<--- Score

121. Are the assumptions believable and achievable?
<--- Score

122. Who is responsible for IT product line?
<--- Score

123. Is there any existing IT product line governance structure?
<--- Score

124. What potential megatrends could make your business model obsolete?
<--- Score

125. What are the short and long-term IT product line goals?
<--- Score

126. What did you miss in the interview for the worst hire you ever made?
<--- Score

127. Why do and why don't your customers like your organization?
<--- Score

128. What happens if you do not have enough funding?
<--- Score

129. How do you determine the key elements that affect IT product line workforce satisfaction, how are these elements determined for different workforce groups and segments?
<--- Score

130. Is the IT product line organization completing tasks effectively and efficiently?
<--- Score

131. How will you motivate the stakeholders with the least vested interest?
<--- Score

132. Are all key stakeholders present at all Structured Walkthroughs?
<--- Score

133. Do you have past IT product line successes?
<--- Score

134. How will you know that the IT product line project has been successful?

<--- Score

135. What are the top 3 things at the forefront of your IT product line agendas for the next 3 years?
<--- Score

136. Are the criteria for selecting recommendations stated?
<--- Score

137. What are the challenges?
<--- Score

138. If you were responsible for initiating and implementing major changes in your organization, what steps might you take to ensure acceptance of those changes?
<--- Score

139. Who do you want your customers to become?
<--- Score

140. Why is IT product line important for you now?
<--- Score

141. Do you think you know, or do you know you know ?
<--- Score

142. Are you making progress, and are you making progress as IT product line leaders?
<--- Score

143. Whose voice (department, ethnic group, women, older workers, etc) might you have missed hearing from in your company, and how might you amplify

this voice to create positive momentum for your business?
<--- Score

144. What is your competitive advantage?
<--- Score

145. Which models, tools and techniques are necessary?
<--- Score

146. How do you keep the momentum going?
<--- Score

147. What may be the consequences for the performance of an organization if all stakeholders are not consulted regarding IT product line?
<--- Score

148. How do you foster the skills, knowledge, talents, attributes, and characteristics you want to have?
<--- Score

149. At what moment would you think; Will I get fired?
<--- Score

150. Are you / should you be revolutionary or evolutionary?
<--- Score

151. Who uses your product in ways you never expected?
<--- Score

Add up total points for this section:

_____ = Total points for this section

Divided by: _____ (number of
statements answered) = _____
Average score for this section

Transfer your score to the IT product
line Index at the beginning of the Self-
Assessment.

IT Product Line and Managing Projects, Criteria for Project Managers:

1.0 Initiating Process Group: IT Product Line

1. Do you understand the quality and control criteria that must be achieved for successful IT Product Line project completion?

2. Have you evaluated the teams performance and asked for feedback?

3. If the risk event occurs, what will you do?

4. Are identified risks being monitored properly, are new risks arising during the IT Product Line project or are foreseen risks occurring?

5. How will you know you did it?

6. How can you make your needs known?

7. Were decisions made in a timely manner?

8. Based on your IT Product Line project communication management plan, what worked well?

9. Who does what?

10. If action is called for, what form should it take?

11. Who is behind the IT Product Line project?

12. Are the IT Product Line project team and stakeholders meeting regularly and using a meeting agenda and taking notes to accurately document

what is being covered and what happened in the weekly meetings?

13. How should needs be met?

14. Do you know if the IT Product Line project requires outside equipment or vendor resources?

15. For technology IT Product Line projects only: Are all production support stakeholders (Business unit, technical support, & user) prepared for implementation with appropriate contingency plans?

16. Are there resources to maintain and support the outcome of the IT Product Line project?

17. How do you help others satisfy needs?

18. What were the challenges that you encountered during the execution of a previous IT Product Line project that you would not want to repeat?

19. The process to Manage Stakeholders is part of which process group?

20. How will it affect me?

1.1 Project Charter: IT Product Line

21. Who manages integration?

22. Dependent IT Product Line projects: what IT Product Line projects must be underway or completed before this IT Product Line project can be successful?

23. Why have you chosen the aim you have set forth?

24. Why do you manage integration?

25. What is the business need?

26. How much?

27. What are the known stakeholder requirements?

28. Why the improvements?

29. Name and describe the elements that deal with providing the detail?

30. What material?

31. Are you building in-house ?

32. Market – identify products market, including whether it is outside of the objective: what is the purpose of the program or IT Product Line project?

33. Why use a IT Product Line project charter?

34. When?

35. Is time of the essence?

36. Must Have?

37. What are the assigned resources?

38. What are some examples of a business case?

39. Fit with other Products Compliments – Cannibalizes?

40. Why is it important?

1.2 Stakeholder Register: IT Product Line

41. Is your organization ready for change?

42. Who is managing stakeholder engagement?

43. What & Why?

44. What is the power of the stakeholder?

45. How much influence do they have on the IT Product Line project?

46. What are the major IT Product Line project milestones requiring communications or providing communications opportunities?

47. How big is the gap?

48. Who are the stakeholders?

49. Who wants to talk about Security?

50. What opportunities exist to provide communications?

51. How should employers make voices heard?

52. How will reports be created?

1.3 Stakeholder Analysis Matrix: IT Product Line

53. Philosophy and values?

54. Vulnerable groups; who are the vulnerable groups that might be affected by the IT Product Line project?

55. Who has control over whom?

56. Why do you need to manage IT Product Line project Risk?

57. What actions can be taken to reduce or mitigate risk?

58. Who will be affected by the work?

59. What obstacles does your organization face?

60. Partnerships, agencies, distribution?

61. Cultural, attitudinal, behavioural?

62. Timescales, deadlines and pressures?

63. Business and product development?

64. Are there different rules or organizational models for men and women?

65. Do recommendations include actions to address any differential distribution of impacts?

66. Does the stakeholder want to be involved or merely need to be informed about the IT Product Line project and its process?

67. Insurmountable weaknesses?

68. How are the threatened IT Product Line project targets being used?

69. What is the issue at stake?

70. Global influences?

71. How do they affect the IT Product Line project and its outcomes?

72. Industry or lifestyle trends?

2.0 Planning Process Group: IT Product Line

73. What business situation is being addressed?

74. Do the partners have sufficient financial capacity to keep up the benefits produced by the programme?

75. When developing the estimates for IT Product Line project phases, you choose to add the individual estimates for the activities that comprise each phase. What type of estimation method are you using?

76. Just how important is your work to the overall success of the IT Product Line project?

77. Is the IT Product Line project supported by national and/or local organizations?

78. What is the critical path for this IT Product Line project, and what is the duration of the critical path?

79. Does the program have follow-up mechanisms (to verify the quality of the products, punctuality of delivery, etc.) to measure progress in the achievement of the envisaged results?

80. If a task is partitionable, is this a sufficient condition to reduce the IT Product Line project duration?

81. First of all, should any action be taken?

82. Mitigate. what will you do to minimize the impact should a risk event occur?

83. In what ways can the governance of the IT Product Line project be improved so that it has greater likelihood of achieving future sustainability?

84. Is the schedule for the set products being met?

85. Have more efficient (sensitive) and appropriate measures been adopted to respond to the political and socio-cultural problems identified?

86. If task x starts two days late, what is the effect on the IT Product Line project end date?

87. Explanation: is what the IT Product Line project intents to solve a hard question?

88. What is a Software Development Life Cycle (SDLC)?

89. Are the necessary foundations in place to ensure the sustainability of the results of the IT Product Line project?

90. How will it affect you?

91. Is the identification of the problems, inequalities and gaps, with respective causes, clear in the IT Product Line project?

92. To what extent have the target population and participants made the activities own, taking an active role in it?

2.1 Project Management Plan: IT Product Line

93. Development trends and opportunities. What if the positive direction and vision of your organization causes expected trends to change?

94. What are the deliverables?

95. If the IT Product Line project management plan is a comprehensive document that guides you in IT Product Line project execution and control, then what should it NOT contain?

96. Does the implementation plan have an appropriate division of responsibilities?

97. If the IT Product Line project is complex or scope is specialized, do you have appropriate and/or qualified staff available to perform the tasks?

98. Why Change?

99. When is a IT Product Line project management plan created?

100. How do you manage time?

101. What is IT Product Line project scope management?

102. Has the selected plan been formulated using cost effectiveness and incremental analysis techniques?

103. Is the engineering content at a feasibility level-of-detail, and is it sufficiently complete, to provide an adequate basis for the baseline cost estimate?

104. Who is the sponsor?

105. What is risk management?

106. Are the proposed IT Product Line project purposes different than a previously authorized IT Product Line project?

107. What is the justification?

108. When is the IT Product Line project management plan created?

109. What are the constraints?

110. Is mitigation authorized or recommended?

111. Is there an incremental analysis/cost effectiveness analysis of proposed mitigation features based on an approved method and using an accepted model?

2.2 Scope Management Plan: IT Product Line

112. Is the steering committee active in IT Product Line project oversight?

113. Have IT Product Line project team accountabilities & responsibilities been clearly defined?

114. Timeline and milestones?

115. Is the schedule updated on a periodic basis?

116. Assess the expected stability of the scope of this IT Product Line project how likely is it to change, how frequently, and by how much?

117. Are measurements and feedback mechanisms incorporated in tracking work effort & refining work estimating techniques?

118. Materials available for performing the work?

119. Are tasks tracked by hours?

120. Have the procedures for identifying variances from estimates & adjusting the detailed work program been followed?

121. Are the existing and future without-plan conditions reasonable and appropriate?

122. Can each item be appropriately scheduled?

123. Are calculations and results of analyzes essentially correct?

124. Are staffing resource estimates sufficiently detailed and documented for use in planning and tracking the IT Product Line project?

125. What should you drop in order to add something new?

126. What are the risks that could significantly affect the resources needed for the IT Product Line project?

127. Are trade-offs between accepting the risk and mitigating the risk identified?

128. Are you spending the right amount of money for specific tasks?

129. For which criterion is it tolerable not to meet the original parameters?

130. Has the IT Product Line project manager been identified?

131. Is there a formal set of procedures supporting Issues Management?

2.3 Requirements Management Plan: IT Product Line

132. Did you use declarative statements?

133. Who will do the reporting and to whom will reports be delivered?

134. Subject to change control?

135. Do you know which stakeholders will participate in the requirements effort?

136. What cost metrics will be used?

137. When and how will a requirements baseline be established in this IT Product Line project?

138. Is there formal agreement on who has authority to approve a change in requirements?

139. How knowledgeable is the team in the proposed application area?

140. Will you perform a Requirements Risk assessment and develop a plan to deal with risks?

141. What is the earliest finish date for this IT Product Line project if it is scheduled to start on ...?

142. Is any organizational data being used or stored?

143. What are you trying to do?

144. What went wrong?

145. After the requirements are gathered and set forth on the requirements register, theyre little more than a laundry list of items. Some may be duplicates, some might conflict with others and some will be too broad or too vague to understand. Describe how the requirements will be analyzed. Who will perform the analysis?

146. Did you provide clear and concise specifications?

147. Will the contractors involved take full responsibility?

148. Have stakeholders been instructed in the Change Control process?

149. Is the system software (non-operating system) new to the IT IT Product Line project team?

150. How will bidders price evaluations be done, by deliverables, phases, or in a big bang?

151. Who will finally present the work or product(s) for acceptance?

2.4 Requirements Documentation: IT Product Line

152. How linear / iterative is your Requirements Gathering process (or will it be)?

153. Where do system and software requirements come from, what are sources?

154. How much testing do you need to do to prove that your system is safe?

155. Completeness. are all functions required by the customer included?

156. How do you know when a Requirement is accurate enough?

157. Where are business rules being captured?

158. Where do you define what is a customer, what are the attributes of customer?

159. What if the system wasn t implemented?

160. Do technical resources exist?

161. What is effective documentation?

162. How do you get the user to tell you what they want?

163. What is a show stopper in the requirements?

164. Can the requirements be checked?

165. How will requirements be documented and who signs off on them?

166. What are the acceptance criteria?

167. Who is interacting with the system?

168. Is the origin of the requirement clearly stated?

169. Is the requirement properly understood?

170. What kind of entity is a problem ?

171. What variations exist for a process?

2.5 Requirements Traceability Matrix: IT Product Line

172. Will you use a Requirements Traceability Matrix?

173. How do you manage scope?

174. What percentage of IT Product Line projects are producing traceability matrices between requirements and other work products?

175. How will it affect the stakeholders personally in career?

176. Is there a requirements traceability process in place?

177. Why do you manage scope?

178. Why use a WBS?

179. What is the WBS?

180. How small is small enough?

181. Do you have a clear understanding of all subcontracts in place?

182. Describe the process for approving requirements so they can be added to the traceability matrix and IT Product Line project work can be performed. Will the IT Product Line project requirements become approved in writing?

183. What are the chronologies, contingencies, consequences, criteria?

2.6 Project Scope Statement: IT Product Line

184. Write a brief purpose statement for this IT Product Line project. Include a business justification statement. What is the product of this IT Product Line project?

185. Is the plan for your organization of the IT Product Line project resources adequate?

186. Will statistics related to QA be collected, trends analyzed, and problems raised as issues?

187. If the scope changes, what will the impact be to your IT Product Line project in terms of duration, cost, quality, or any other important areas of the IT Product Line project?

188. Once its defined, what is the stability of the IT Product Line project scope?

189. If you were to write a list of what should not be included in the scope statement, what are the things that you would recommend be described as out-of-scope?

190. How often do you estimate that the scope might change, and why?

191. What are the possible consequences should a risk come to occur?

192. Where and how does the team fit within your organization structure?

193. Is the IT Product Line project manager qualified and experienced in IT Product Line project management?

194. Will the risk status be reported to management on a regular and frequent basis?

195. Relevant - ask yourself can you get there; why are you doing this IT Product Line project?

196. Will the risk documents be filed?

197. Has a method and process for requirement tracking been developed?

198. Is the quality function identified and assigned?

199. Is an issue management process documented and filed?

200. Do you anticipate new stakeholders joining the IT Product Line project over time?

201. Is the scope of your IT Product Line project well defined?

202. Are there issues that could affect the existing requirements for the result, service, or product if the scope changes?

2.7 Assumption and Constraint Log: IT Product Line

203. Are formal code reviews conducted?

204. Does the system design reflect the requirements?

205. What is positive about the current process?

206. Are requirements management tracking tools and procedures in place?

207. Does the document/deliverable meet all requirements (for example, statement of work) specific to this deliverable?

208. Does the document/deliverable meet general requirements (for example, statement of work) for all deliverables?

209. How can you prevent/fix violations?

210. Are processes for release management of new development from coding and unit testing, to integration testing, to training, and production defined and followed?

211. When can log be discarded?

212. Should factors be unpredictable over time?

213. No superfluous information or marketing narrative?

214. Are there processes in place to ensure that all the terms and code concepts have been documented consistently?

215. Have IT Product Line project management standards and procedures been established and documented?

216. What do you audit?

217. Model-building: what data-analytic strategies are useful when building proportional-hazards models?

218. Is there adequate stakeholder participation for the vetting of requirements definition, changes and management?

219. Does the traceability documentation describe the tool and/or mechanism to be used to capture traceability throughout the life cycle?

220. Have all involved stakeholders and work groups committed to the IT Product Line project?

221. What worked well?

222. How are new requirements or changes to requirements identified?

2.8 Work Breakdown Structure: IT Product Line

223. How big is a work-package?

224. Is the work breakdown structure (wbs) defined and is the scope of the IT Product Line project clear with assigned deliverable owners?

225. When would you develop a Work Breakdown Structure?

226. Who has to do it?

227. Where does it take place?

228. Is it still viable?

229. What is the probability that the IT Product Line project duration will exceed xx weeks?

230. What is the probability of completing the IT Product Line project in less that xx days?

231. Can you make it?

232. When do you stop?

233. How will you and your IT Product Line project team define the IT Product Line projects scope and work breakdown structure?

234. When does it have to be done?

235. How far down?

236. Is it a change in scope?

237. Why would you develop a Work Breakdown Structure?

238. How many levels?

239. How much detail?

2.9 WBS Dictionary: IT Product Line

240. What went right?

241. Software specification, development, integration, and testing, licenses ?

242. Are significant decision points, constraints, and interfaces identified as key milestones?

243. Does the contractors system provide for determination of price variance by comparing planned Vs actual commitments?

244. Incurrence of actual indirect costs in excess of budgets, by element of expense?

245. Identify and isolate causes of favorable and unfavorable cost and schedule variances?

246. Is undistributed budget limited to contract effort which cannot yet be planned to CWBS elements at or below the level specified for reporting to the Government?

247. Actual cost of work performed?

248. Are the responsibilities and authorities of each of the above organizational elements or managers clearly defined?

249. All cwbs elements specified for external reporting?

250. Is the entire contract planned in time-phased control accounts to the extent practicable?

251. Do the lines of authority for incurring indirect costs correspond to the lines of responsibility for management control of the same components of costs?

252. Are detailed work packages planned as far in advance as practicable?

253. Performance to date and material commitment?

254. Are the variances between budgeted and actual indirect costs identified and analyzed at the level of assigned responsibility for control (indirect pool, department, etc.)?

255. Does the accounting system provide a basis for auditing records of direct costs chargeable to the contract?

256. Where engineering standards or other internal work measurement systems are used, is there a formal relationship between corresponding values and work package budgets?

257. Where learning is used in developing underlying budgets is there a direct relationship between anticipated learning and time phased budgets?

258. Are work packages assigned to performing organizations?

259. Does the contractors system include procedures for measuring performance of the lowest level

organization responsible for the control account?

2.10 Schedule Management Plan: IT Product Line

260. Does the IT Product Line project have quality set of schedule BOEs?

261. Are the predecessor and successor relationships accurate?

262. Is a process for scheduling and reporting defined, including forms and formats?

263. Have the key functions and capabilities been defined and assigned to each release or iteration?

264. Are post milestone IT Product Line project reviews (PMPR) conducted with your organization at least once a year?

265. Is IT Product Line project status reviewed with the steering and executive teams at appropriate intervals?

266. Are software metrics formally captured, analyzed and used as a basis for other IT Product Line project estimates?

267. Is current scope of the IT Product Line project substantially different than that originally defined?

268. Are risk oriented checklists used during risk identification?

269. Are staff skills known and available for each task?

270. What weaknesses do you have?

271. Have the key elements of a coherent IT Product Line project management strategy been established?

272. Is there a formal process for updating the IT Product Line project baseline?

273. Is there any form of automated support for Issues Management?

274. Has the schedule been baselined?

275. Were IT Product Line project team members involved in detailed estimating and scheduling?

276. Has a IT Product Line project Communications Plan been developed?

277. What will be the format of the schedule model?

278. What tools and techniques will be used to estimate activity resources?

2.11 Activity List: IT Product Line

279. Can you determine the activity that must finish, before this activity can start?

280. Are the required resources available or need to be acquired?

281. How do you determine the late start (LS) for each activity?

282. How much slack is available in the IT Product Line project?

283. When do the individual activities need to start and finish?

284. Who will perform the work?

285. How detailed should a IT Product Line project get?

286. Is there anything planned that does not need to be here?

287. What went well?

288. In what sequence?

289. What will be performed?

290. What are the critical bottleneck activities?

291. Is infrastructure setup part of your IT Product

Line project?

292. What is the total time required to complete the IT Product Line project if no delays occur?

293. How can the IT Product Line project be displayed graphically to better visualize the activities?

294. What did not go as well?

295. How should ongoing costs be monitored to try to keep the IT Product Line project within budget?

296. For other activities, how much delay can be tolerated?

297. How will it be performed?

298. What is the LF and LS for each activity?

2.12 Activity Attributes: IT Product Line

299. Which method produces the more accurate cost assignment?

300. Is there a trend during the year?

301. Has management defined a definite timeframe for the turnaround or IT Product Line project window?

302. Resources to accomplish the work?

303. Time for overtime?

304. Does your organization of the data change its meaning?

305. What is your organizations history in doing similar activities?

306. How much activity detail is required?

307. What is missing?

308. Have you identified the Activity Leveling Priority code value on each activity?

309. Activity: fair or not fair?

310. Were there other ways you could have organized the data to achieve similar results?

311. How many resources do you need to complete the work scope within a limit of X number of days?

312. Why?

313. Activity: what is In the Bag?

314. Can more resources be added?

2.13 Milestone List: IT Product Line

315. What is the market for your technology, product or service?

316. It is to be a narrative text providing the crucial aspects of your IT Product Line project proposal answering what, who, how, when and where?

317. Loss of key staff?

318. Describe the concept of the technology, product or service that will be or has been developed. How will it be used?

319. How late can the activity finish?

320. When will the IT Product Line project be complete?

321. Describe your organizations strengths and core competencies. What factors will make your organization succeed?

322. Own known vulnerabilities?

323. How will the milestone be verified?

324. How will you get the word out to customers?

325. Sustaining internal capabilities?

326. What are your competitors vulnerabilities?

327. Milestone pages should display the UserID of the person who added the milestone. Does a report or query exist that provides this audit information?

328. Which path is the critical path?

329. Identify critical paths (one or more) and which activities are on the critical path?

330. How soon can the activity start?

331. Legislative effects?

2.14 Network Diagram: IT Product Line

332. What are the tools?

333. What are the Key Success Factors?

334. What to do and When?

335. What are the Major Administrative Issues?

336. Planning: who, how long, what to do?

337. Will crashing x weeks return more in benefits than it costs?

338. What activity must be completed immediately before this activity can start?

339. If the IT Product Line project network diagram cannot change and you have extra personnel resources, what is the BEST thing to do?

340. Are you on time?

341. What is the probability of completing the IT Product Line project in less that xx days?

342. Review the logical flow of the network diagram. Take a look at which activities you have first and then sequence the activities. Do they make sense?

343. What job or jobs precede it?

344. What job or jobs could run concurrently?

345. Where do you schedule uncertainty time?

346. What must be completed before an activity can be started?

347. What controls the start and finish of a job?

348. Are the required resources available?

349. Where do schedules come from?

2.15 Activity Resource Requirements: IT Product Line

350. What is the Work Plan Standard?

351. Organizational Applicability?

352. How do you handle petty cash?

353. How many signatures do you require on a check and does this match what is in your policy and procedures?

354. Which logical relationship does the PDM use most often?

355. Anything else?

356. Are there unresolved issues that need to be addressed?

357. Why do you do that?

358. Other support in specific areas?

359. When does monitoring begin?

360. Do you use tools like decomposition and rolling-wave planning to produce the activity list and other outputs?

361. What are constraints that you might find during the Human Resource Planning process?

2.16 Resource Breakdown Structure: IT Product Line

362. Why is this important?

363. Who needs what information?

364. Goals for the IT Product Line project. What is each stakeholders desired outcome for the IT Product Line project?

365. What defines a successful IT Product Line project?

366. Is predictive resource analysis being done?

367. Who is allowed to perform which functions?

368. Which resource planning tool provides information on resource responsibility and accountability?

369. What is each stakeholders desired outcome for the IT Product Line project?

370. What is the difference between % Complete and % work?

371. Who will be used as a IT Product Line project team member?

372. Why do you do it?

373. How should the information be delivered?

374. What is the number one predictor of a groups productivity?

375. The list could probably go on, but, the thing that you would most like to know is, How long & How much?

376. Who will use the system?

377. What defines a successful IT Product Line project?

2.17 Activity Duration Estimates: IT Product Line

378. Briefly describe some key events in the history of IT Product Line project management. What IT Product Line project was the first to use modern IT Product Line project management?

379. It under budget or over budget?

380. What are some crucial elements of a good IT Product Line project plan?

381. Which skills do you think are most important for an information technology IT Product Line project manager?

382. Do you agree with the suggestions provided for improving IT Product Line project communications?

383. Is the work performed reviewed against contractual objectives?

384. Why is there a growing trend in outsourcing, especially in the government?

385. How could you define throughput and how would your organization benefit from maximizing it?

386. (Cpi), and schedule performance index (spi) for the IT Product Line project?

387. Who will be the main sponsor for it?

388. Account for the make-or-buy process and how to perform the financial calculations involved in the process. What are the main types of contracts if you do decide to outsource?

389. Are IT Product Line project management tools and techniques consistently applied throughout all IT Product Line projects?

390. Which suggestions do you find most useful?

391. Is a IT Product Line project charter created once a IT Product Line project is formally recognized?

392. What is wrong with this scenario?

393. Is a contract developed which obligates the seller and the buyer?

394. Will the new application negatively affect the current IT infrastructure?

395. Have most organizations benefited from outsourcing?

396. What is pmp certification, and why do you think the number of people earning it has grown so much in the past ten years?

2.18 Duration Estimating Worksheet: IT Product Line

397. What utility impacts are there?

398. When, then?

399. Why estimate time and cost?

400. What is cost and IT Product Line project cost management?

401. Do any colleagues have experience with your organization and/or RFPs?

402. Value pocket identification & quantification what are value pockets?

403. What is next?

404. How should ongoing costs be monitored to try to keep the IT Product Line project within budget?

405. Small or large IT Product Line project?

406. Can the IT Product Line project be constructed as planned?

407. How can the IT Product Line project be displayed graphically to better visualize the activities?

408. Will the IT Product Line project collaborate with the local community and leverage resources?

409. What is the total time required to complete the IT Product Line project if no delays occur?

410. When does your organization expect to be able to complete it?

411. What questions do you have?

412. Done before proceeding with this activity or what can be done concurrently?

2.19 Project Schedule: IT Product Line

413. Why do you need to manage IT Product Line project Risk?

414. Should you include sub-activities?

415. Are quality inspections and review activities listed in the IT Product Line project schedule(s)?

416. Was the IT Product Line project schedule reviewed by all stakeholders and formally accepted?

417. Change management required?

418. Should you have a test for each code module?

419. If there are any qualifying green components to this IT Product Line project, what portion of the total IT Product Line project cost is green?

420. The wbs is developed as part of a joint planning session. and how do you know that youhave done this right?

421. How detailed should a IT Product Line project get?

422. What is the difference?

423. Does the condition or event threaten the IT Product Line projects objectives in any ways?

424. Meet requirements?

425. Why do you need schedules?

426. How can you address that situation?

427. How can you fix it?

428. How do you know that youhave done this right?

429. Did the IT Product Line project come in on schedule?

430. Why do you think schedule issues often cause the most conflicts on IT Product Line projects?

431. Is infrastructure setup part of your IT Product Line project?

2.20 Cost Management Plan: IT Product Line

432. Responsibilities – what is the split of responsibilities between the owner and contractors?

433. Eac -estimate at completion, what is the total job expected to cost?

434. Will the earned value reporting interface between time and cost management?

435. Are the quality tools and methods identified in the Quality Plan appropriate to the IT Product Line project?

436. Have the key elements of a coherent IT Product Line project management strategy been established?

437. Are vendor invoices audited for accuracy before payment?

438. Contracting method – what contracting method is to be used for the contracts?

439. For cost control purposes?

440. How do you manage cost?

441. What strengths do you have?

442. Is the IT Product Line project sponsor clearly communicating the business case or rationale for why

this IT Product Line project is needed?

443. Is there an onboarding process in place?

444. Are key risk mitigation strategies added to the IT Product Line project schedule?

445. What threats might prevent you from getting there?

446. Does the resource management plan include a personnel development plan?

447. Are enough systems & user personnel assigned to the IT Product Line project?

448. Are quality inspections and review activities listed in the IT Product Line project schedule(s)?

449. Are the appropriate IT resources adequate to meet planned commitments?

2.21 Activity Cost Estimates: IT Product Line

450. What makes a good expected result statement?

451. Was the consultant knowledgeable about the program?

452. What is the IT Product Line projects sustainability strategy that will ensure IT Product Line project results will endure or be sustained?

453. Certification of actual expenditures?

454. What is the activity recast of the budget?

455. Were you satisfied with the work?

456. How and when do you enter into IT Product Line project Procurement Management?

457. Can you delete activities or make them inactive?

458. Scope statement only direct or indirect costs as well?

459. Does the estimator have experience?

460. What cost data should be used to estimate costs during the 2-year follow-up period?

461. What is a IT Product Line project Management Plan?

462. Does the activity use a common approach or business function to deliver its results?

463. Who determines the quality and expertise of contractors?

464. Were the costs or charges reasonable?

465. Is there anything unique in this IT Product Line projects scope statement that will affect resources?

466. How do you do activity recasts?

467. Did the IT Product Line project team have the right skills?

2.22 Cost Estimating Worksheet: IT Product Line

468. What costs are to be estimated?

469. Is it feasible to establish a control group arrangement?

470. What will others want?

471. Will the IT Product Line project collaborate with the local community and leverage resources?

472. What additional IT Product Line project(s) could be initiated as a result of this IT Product Line project?

473. Does the IT Product Line project provide innovative ways for stakeholders to overcome obstacles or deliver better outcomes?

474. Identify the timeframe necessary to monitor progress and collect data to determine how the selected measure has changed?

475. What is the purpose of estimating?

476. What info is needed?

477. Is the IT Product Line project responsive to community need?

478. Who is best positioned to know and assist in identifying corresponding factors?

479. How will the results be shared and to whom?

480. What is the estimated labor cost today based upon this information?

481. Ask: are others positioned to know, are others credible, and will others cooperate?

482. Can a trend be established from historical performance data on the selected measure and are the criteria for using trend analysis or forecasting methods met?

483. What can be included?

484. What happens to any remaining funds not used?

2.23 Cost Baseline: IT Product Line

485. Where do changes come from?

486. Have the lessons learned been filed with the IT Product Line project Management Office?

487. What deliverables come first?

488. Are you meeting with your team regularly?

489. Pcs for your new business. what would the life cycle costs be?

490. Definition of done can be traced back to the definitions of what are you providing to the customer in terms of deliverables?

491. IT Product Line project goals -should others be reconsidered?

492. What would the life cycle costs be?

493. Impact to environment?

494. Is the requested change request a result of changes in other IT Product Line project(s)?

495. What is your organizations history in doing similar tasks?

496. Have the resources used by the IT Product Line project been reassigned to other units or IT Product Line projects?

497. Has the documentation relating to operation and maintenance of the product(s) or service(s) been delivered to, and accepted by, operations management?

498. Has operations management formally accepted responsibility for operating and maintaining the product(s) or service(s) delivered by the IT Product Line project?

499. How likely is it to go wrong?

500. Has the appropriate access to relevant data and analysis capability been granted?

501. Should a more thorough impact analysis be conducted?

502. Has training and knowledge transfer of the operations organization been completed?

2.24 Quality Management Plan: IT Product Line

503. How does your organization ensure the quality, reliability, and user-friendliness of its hardware and software?

504. How do you decide what information to record?

505. Documented results available?

506. How are your organizations compensation and recognition approaches and the performance management system used to reinforce high performance?

507. Are there trends or hot spots?

508. What are your organizations key processes (product, service, business, and support)?

509. Can the requirements be traced to the appropriate components of the solution, as well as test scripts?

510. Would impacts defined serve as impediments?

511. Are there ways to reduce the time it takes to get something approved?

512. How does your organization recruit, hire, and retain new employees?

513. Have IT Product Line project management standards and procedures been established and documented?

514. Who is responsible for approving the qapp?

515. Show/provide copy of procedures for taking field notes?

516. What changes can you make that will result in improvement?

517. What are you trying to accomplish?

518. Contradictory information between document sections?

519. How will you know that a change is actually an improvement?

520. Results Available?

521. Were there any deficiencies / issues identified in the prior years self-assessment?

2.25 Quality Metrics: IT Product Line

522. How do you know if everyone is trying to improve the right things?

523. Is the reporting frequency appropriate?

524. What percentage are outcome-based?

525. What is the benchmark?

526. Which report did you use to create the data you are submitting?

527. Was the overall quality better or worse than previous products?

528. Is there a set of procedures to capture, analyze and act on quality metrics?

529. Is quality culture a competitive advantage?

530. What happens if you get an abnormal result?

531. How effective are your security tests?

532. Where did complaints, returns and warranty claims come from?

533. Subjective quality component: customer satisfaction, how do you measure it?

534. What does this tell us?

535. How is it being measured?

536. Has risk analysis been adequately reviewed?

537. What do you measure?

538. How are requirements conflicts resolved?

539. If the defect rate during testing is substantially higher than that of the previous release (or a similar product), then ask: Did you plan for and actually improve testing effectiveness?

540. Have risk areas been identified?

2.26 Process Improvement Plan: IT Product Line

541. Does explicit definition of the measures exist?

542. Does your process ensure quality?

543. Are you making progress on the improvement framework?

544. Who should prepare the process improvement action plan?

545. Has the time line required to move measurement results from the points of collection to databases or users been established?

546. To elicit goal statements, do you ask a question such as, What do you want to achieve?

547. How do you measure?

548. Where do you want to be?

549. What personnel are the champions for the initiative?

550. Purpose of goal: the motive is determined by asking, why do you want to achieve this goal?

551. Have the supporting tools been developed or acquired?

552. Are you making progress on the goals?

553. What is quality and how will you ensure it?

554. What personnel are the sponsors for that initiative?

555. Management commitment at all levels?

556. What makes people good SPI coaches?

557. What is the test-cycle concept?

558. What lessons have you learned so far?

559. Has a process guide to collect the data been developed?

2.27 Responsibility Assignment Matrix: IT Product Line

560. Can the contractor substantiate work package and planning package budgets?

561. Does each role with Accountable responsibility have the authority within your organization to make the required decisions?

562. What are some important IT Product Line project communications management tools?

563. IT Product Line projected economic escalation?

564. Is the anticipated (firm and potential) business base IT Product Line projected in a rational, consistent manner?

565. Does the contractor use objective results, design reviews, and tests to trace schedule?

566. Ideas for developing soft skills at your organization?

567. Identify potential or actual overruns and underruns?

568. Is it safe to say you can handle more work or that some tasks you are supposed to do arent worth doing?

569. What do you need to implement earned value

management?

570. Are too many reports done in writing instead of verbally?

571. What expertise is available in your department?

572. Most people let you know when others re too busy, and are others really too busy?

573. Is budgeted cost for work performed calculated in a manner consistent with the way work is planned?

574. Are there any drawbacks to using a responsibility assignment matrix?

2.28 Roles and Responsibilities: IT Product Line

575. Is the data complete?

576. How is your work-life balance?

577. What should you highlight for improvement?

578. Is feedback clearly communicated and non-judgmental?

579. Was the expectation clearly communicated?

580. Do the values and practices inherent in the culture of your organization foster or hinder the process?

581. What should you do now to ensure that you are meeting all expectations of your current position?

582. Are your budgets supportive of a culture of quality data?

583. Required skills, knowledge, experience?

584. Are governance roles and responsibilities documented?

585. What is working well within your organizations performance management system?

586. Does your vision/mission support a culture of

quality data?

587. Who is responsible for implementation activities and where will the functions, roles and responsibilities be defined?

588. Concern: where are you limited or have no authority, where you can not influence?

589. How well did the IT Product Line project Team understand the expectations of specific roles and responsibilities?

590. Are IT Product Line project team roles and responsibilities identified and documented?

591. What areas of supervision are challenging for you?

592. What areas would you highlight for changes or improvements?

593. Once the responsibilities are defined for the IT Product Line project, have the deliverables, roles and responsibilities been clearly communicated to every participant?

594. Have you ever been a part of this team?

2.29 Human Resource Management Plan: IT Product Line

595. Are IT Product Line project team roles and responsibilities identified and documented?

596. Does the IT Product Line project have a Quality Culture?

597. Do people have the competencies to meet the strategic objectives?

598. What talent is needed?

599. Is quality monitored from the perspective of the customers needs and expectations?

600. Quality assurance overheads?

601. Are people being developed to meet the challenges of the future?

602. Were sponsors and decision makers available when needed outside regularly scheduled meetings?

603. Do you have the reasons why the changes to your organizational systems and capabilities are required?

604. How complete is the human resource management plan?

605. Is there general agreement & acceptance of the

current status and progress of the IT Product Line project?

606. Identify who is needed on the core IT Product Line project team to complete IT Product Line project deliverables and achieve its goals and objectives. What skills, knowledge and experiences are required?

607. Are quality metrics defined?

608. Are status reports received per the IT Product Line project Plan?

609. Personnel with expertise?

610. Are multiple estimation methods being employed?

611. How relevant is this attribute to this IT Product Line project or audit?

612. Have stakeholder accountabilities & responsibilities been clearly defined?

613. What are the Staffing Requirements?

614. Are target dates established for each milestone deliverable?

2.30 Communications Management Plan: IT Product Line

615. Who were proponents/opponents?

616. Is there an important stakeholder who is actively opposed and will not receive messages?

617. How much time does it take to do it?

618. Will messages be directly related to the release strategy or phases of the IT Product Line project?

619. What data is going to be required?

620. Why is stakeholder engagement important?

621. Are the stakeholders getting the information others need, are others consulted, are concerns addressed?

622. Who needs to know and how much?

623. What approaches do you use?

624. Which stakeholders can influence others?

625. Are stakeholders internal or external?

626. Are others needed?

627. What is the stakeholders level of authority?

628. Do you then often overlook a key stakeholder or stakeholder group?

629. What communications method?

630. How do you manage communications?

631. What steps can you take for a positive relationship?

632. Do you feel more overwhelmed by stakeholders?

633. Who is involved as you identify stakeholders?

2.31 Risk Management Plan: IT Product Line

634. Was an original risk assessment/risk management plan completed?

635. What things are likely to change?

636. Is security a central objective?

637. Are you on schedule?

638. Are requirements fully understood by the software engineering team and customers?

639. What risks are necessary to achieve success?

640. Workarounds are determined during which step of risk management?

641. Market risk -will the new service or product be useful to your organization or marketable to others?

642. Have staff received necessary training?

643. What would you do?

644. Do requirements demand the use of new analysis, design, or testing methods?

645. What does a risk management program do?

646. Is the process being followed?

647. Which risks should get the attention?

648. What did not work so well?

649. What is the cost to the IT Product Line project if it does occur?

650. Are flexibility and reuse paramount?

651. Do requirements put excessive performance constraints on the product?

652. Are the required plans included, such as nonstructural flood risk management plans?

653. Can it be changed quickly?

2.32 Risk Register: IT Product Line

654. Manageability – have mitigations to the risk been identified?

655. Risk categories: what are the main categories of risks that should be addressed on this IT Product Line project?

656. What could prevent you delivering on the strategic program objectives and what is being done to mitigate corresponding issues?

657. How are risks identified?

658. Risk documentation: what reporting formats and processes will be used for risk management activities?

659. Having taken action, how did the responses effect change, and where is the IT Product Line project now?

660. What action, if any, has been taken to respond to the risk?

661. When will it happen?

662. Severity Prediction?

663. Which key risks have ineffective responses or outstanding improvement actions?

664. Methodology: how will risk management be performed on this IT Product Line project?

665. Are your objectives at risk?

666. What can be done about it?

667. People risk -are people with appropriate skills available to help complete the IT Product Line project?

668. What may happen or not go according to plan?

669. Assume the event happens, what is the Most Likely impact?

670. Amongst the action plans and recommendations that you have to introduce are there some that could stop or delay the overall program?

671. What are your key risks/show istoppers and what is being done to manage them?

672. User involvement: do you have the right users?

673. Who is going to do it?

2.33 Probability and Impact Assessment: IT Product Line

674. What are the probabilities of chosen technologies being suitable for local conditions?

675. How is the risk management process used in practice?

676. What will be cost of redeployment of personnel?

677. What is the IT Product Line project managers level of commitment and professionalism?

678. Are the risk data complete?

679. Can the IT Product Line project proceed without assuming the risk?

680. What are the chances the risk event will occur?

681. What are the industrial relations prevailing in your organization?

682. How well is the risk understood?

683. Are testing tools available and suitable?

684. Is there additional information that would make you more confident about your analysis?

685. What are the current requirements of the customer?

686. How would you suggest monitoring for risk transition indicators?

687. Do you have specific methods that you use for each phase of the process?

688. How do risks change during a IT Product Line project life cycle?

689. What risks does your organization have if the IT Product Line projects fail to meet deadline?

690. Who has experience with this?

691. Are formal technical reviews part of this process?

692. Are trained personnel, including supervisors and IT Product Line project managers, available to handle such a large IT Product Line project?

693. How do you define a risk?

2.34 Probability and Impact Matrix: IT Product Line

694. What are the current or emerging trends of culture?

695. How do you analyze the risks in the different types of IT Product Line projects?

696. How solid are the price-volume IT Product Line projections?

697. What is the level of experience available with your organization?

698. What should be the level of coordination?

699. The customer requests a change to the IT Product Line project that would increase the IT Product Line project risk. Which should you do before ass the others?

700. Can you avoid altogether some things that might go wrong?

701. Do end-users have realistic expectations?

702. Is the technology to be built new to your organization?

703. How will economic events and trends likely affect the IT Product Line project?

704. Can you handle the investment risk?

705. Non-valid or incredible information?

706. Are you working on the right risks?

707. Which phase of the IT Product Line project do you take part in?

708. What should be the level of difficulty in handling the technology?

2.35 Risk Data Sheet: IT Product Line

709. Has a sensitivity analysis been carried out?

710. What is the chance that it will happen?

711. How do you handle product safely?

712. Risk of what?

713. Are new hazards created?

714. Do effective diagnostic tests exist?

715. Whom do you serve (customers)?

716. What will be the consequences if it happens?

717. What is the environment within which you operate (social trends, economic, community values, broad based participation, national directions etc.)?

718. How reliable is the data source?

719. What will be the consequences if the risk happens?

720. Will revised controls lead to tolerable risk levels?

721. What are you trying to achieve (Objectives)?

722. What are the main threats to your existence?

723. What are your core values?

724. What were the Causes that contributed?

725. What was measured?

726. Potential for recurrence?

2.36 Procurement Management Plan: IT Product Line

727. Are the schedule estimates reasonable given the IT Product Line project?

728. Have all involved IT Product Line project stakeholders and work groups committed to the IT Product Line project?

729. Has the IT Product Line project scope been baselined?

730. Have reserves been created to address risks?

731. Do IT Product Line project managers participating in the IT Product Line project know the IT Product Line projects true status first hand?

732. Were escalated issues resolved promptly?

733. Are vendor contract reports, reviews and visits conducted periodically?

734. What types of contracts will be used?

735. Are action items captured and managed?

736. Are meeting minutes captured and sent out after meetings?

737. Is there a formal set of procedures supporting Stakeholder Management?

738. Are any non-compliance issues that exist communicated to your organization?

739. Is stakeholder involvement adequate?

740. Has your organization readiness assessment been conducted?

741. Are cause and effect determined for risks when others occur?

742. Have key stakeholders been identified?

743. Is the structure for tracking the IT Product Line project schedule well defined and assigned to a specific individual?

2.37 Source Selection Criteria: IT Product Line

744. Have team members been adequately trained?

745. Do you want to wait until all offerors have been evaluated?

746. What are the requirements for publicizing a RFP?

747. What should be considered?

748. Are considerations anticipated?

749. Is a letter of commitment from each proposed team member and key subcontractor included?

750. What should be considered when developing evaluation standards?

751. Do you ensure you evaluate what you asked for, not what you want to see or expect to see?

752. What information is to be provided and when should it be provided?

753. Is the offeror pricing what is technically proposed?

754. What should a DRFP include?

755. What can not be disclosed?

756. How much past performance information should be requested?

757. What is cost analysis and when should it be performed?

758. Are there any specific considerations that precludes offers from being selected as the awardee?

759. What should be the contracting officers strategy?

760. Who is entitled to a debriefing?

761. Comparison of each offers prices to the estimated prices -are there significant differences?

2.38 Stakeholder Management Plan: IT Product Line

762. Is the process working, and are people executing in compliance of the process?

763. Are updated IT Product Line project time & resource estimates reasonable based on the current IT Product Line project stage?

764. Does the IT Product Line project have a formal IT Product Line project Charter?

765. Is IT Product Line project status reviewed with the steering and executive teams at appropriate intervals?

766. Is the assigned IT Product Line project manager a PMP (Certified IT Product Line project manager) and experienced?

767. Are metrics used to evaluate and manage Vendors?

768. Which risks pose the highest threat?

769. Is the performance of the supplier to be rated and documented?

770. What is meant by managing the triple constraint?

771. What other teams / processes would be impacted by changes to the current process, and how?

772. Is the current scope of the IT Product Line project substantially different than that originally defined?

773. Who is responsible for gathering and reporting data for employment?

774. Were the budget estimates reasonable?

775. What are the advantages and disadvantages of using external contracted resources?

776. What conditions make using three-point estimating justifiable?

777. Describe the process that will be used to design, develop, review, accept, distribute and change outputs. Will all outputs delivered by the IT Product Line project follow the same process?

2.39 Change Management Plan: IT Product Line

778. Who will fund the training?

779. What skills, education, knowledge, or work experiences should the resources have for each identified competency?

780. What are the dependencies?

781. Do you need new systems?

782. Who will be the change levers?

783. Have the business unit contacts been selected and notified?

784. What is the reason for the communication?

785. What is going to be done differently?

786. Is there a need for new relationships to be built?

787. What communication network would you use – informal or formal?

788. What work practices will be affected?

789. What policies and procedures need to be changed?

790. Who should be involved in developing a change

management strategy?

791. How much IT Product Line project management is needed?

792. When does it make sense to customize?

793. Does this change represent a completely new process for your organization, or a different application of an existing process?

794. Are work location changes required?

795. How will you deal with anger about the restricting of communications due to confidentiality considerations?

796. What did the people around you say about it?

797. What prerequisite knowledge do corresponding groups need?

3.0 Executing Process Group: IT Product Line

798. How can software assist in IT Product Line project communications?

799. Will a new application be developed using existing hardware, software, and networks?

800. What were things that you need to improve?

801. Measurable - are the targets measurable?

802. How well did the chosen processes produce the expected results?

803. What are the critical steps involved with strategy mapping?

804. What IT Product Line projects and services are in the portfolio of your organization?

805. What is the difference between using brainstorming and the Delphi technique for risk identification?

806. What were things that you did very well and want to do the same again on the next IT Product Line project?

807. Just how important is your work to the overall success of the IT Product Line project?

808. How do you control progress of your IT Product Line project?

809. Would you rate yourself as being risk-averse, risk-neutral, or risk-seeking?

810. How is IT Product Line project performance information created and distributed?

811. Will additional funds be needed for hardware or software?

812. How can your organization use a weighted decision matrix to evaluate proposals as part of source selection?

813. When is the appropriate time to bring the scorecard to Board meetings?

814. What is the shortest possible time it will take to complete this IT Product Line project?

815. Do schedule issues conflicts?

3.1 Team Member Status Report: IT Product Line

816. How much risk is involved?

817. Does every department have to have a IT Product Line project Manager on staff?

818. Will the staff do training or is that done by a third party?

819. Does the product, good, or service already exist within your organization?

820. How will resource planning be done?

821. Why is it to be done?

822. How can you make it practical?

823. Are the attitudes of staff regarding IT Product Line project work improving?

824. Do you have an Enterprise IT Product Line project Management Office (EPMO)?

825. How it is to be done?

826. The problem with Reward & Recognition Programs is that the truly deserving people all too often get left out. How can you make it practical?

827. What is to be done?

828. How does this product, good, or service meet the needs of the IT Product Line project and your organization as a whole?

829. Is there evidence that staff is taking a more professional approach toward management of your organizations IT Product Line projects?

830. Are your organizations IT Product Line projects more successful over time?

831. What specific interest groups do you have in place?

832. When a teams productivity and success depend on collaboration and the efficient flow of information, what generally fails them?

833. Does your organization have the means (staff, money, contract, etc.) to produce or to acquire the product, good, or service?

834. Are the products of your organizations IT Product Line projects meeting customers objectives?

3.2 Change Request: IT Product Line

835. What kind of information about the change request needs to be captured?

836. Have scm procedures for noting the change, recording it, and reporting it been followed?

837. What are the requirements for urgent changes?

838. For which areas does this operating procedure apply?

839. What mechanism is used to appraise others of changes that are made?

840. Why do you want to have a change control system?

841. How fast will change requests be approved?

842. What should be regulated in a change control operating instruction?

843. What are the Impacts to your organization?

844. Who is responsible to authorize changes?

845. Who needs to approve change requests?

846. Since there are no change requests in your IT Product Line project at this point, what must you have before you begin?

847. Is it feasible to use requirements attributes as predictors of reliability?

848. Who is responsible for the implementation and monitoring of all measures?

849. Can static requirements change attributes like the size of the change be used to predict reliability in execution?

850. Who is included in the change control team?

851. How does a team identify the discrete elements of a configuration?

852. What is a Change Request Form?

3.3 Change Log: IT Product Line

853. Will the IT Product Line project fail if the change request is not executed?

854. How does this relate to the standards developed for specific business processes?

855. Is the submitted change a new change or a modification of a previously approved change?

856. Is the change request open, closed or pending?

857. Is the change request within IT Product Line project scope?

858. Does the suggested change request represent a desired enhancement to the products functionality?

859. Is the change backward compatible without limitations?

860. Does the suggested change request seem to represent a necessary enhancement to the product?

861. When was the request submitted?

862. Do the described changes impact on the integrity or security of the system?

863. How does this change affect the timeline of the schedule?

864. Is this a mandatory replacement?

865. How does this change affect scope?

866. Who initiated the change request?

867. When was the request approved?

868. Is the requested change request a result of changes in other IT Product Line project(s)?

3.4 Decision Log: IT Product Line

869. With whom was the decision shared or considered?

870. Which variables make a critical difference?

871. How consolidated and comprehensive a story can you tell by capturing currently available incident data in a central location and through a log of key decisions during an incident?

872. What alternatives/risks were considered?

873. At what point in time does loss become unacceptable?

874. What is the average size of your matters in an applicable measurement?

875. Linked to original objective?

876. What are the cost implications?

877. What eDiscovery problem or issue did your organization set out to fix or make better?

878. How effective is maintaining the log at facilitating organizational learning?

879. It becomes critical to track and periodically revisit both operational effectiveness; Are you noticing all that you need to, and are you interpreting what you see effectively?

880. Is everything working as expected?

881. What is the line where eDiscovery ends and document review begins?

882. Does anything need to be adjusted?

883. Meeting purpose; why does this team meet?

884. Do strategies and tactics aimed at less than full control reduce the costs of management or simply shift the cost burden?

885. How does provision of information, both in terms of content and presentation, influence acceptance of alternative strategies?

886. What makes you different or better than others companies selling the same thing?

887. How does an increasing emphasis on cost containment influence the strategies and tactics used?

888. Is your opponent open to a non-traditional workflow, or will it likely challenge anything you do?

3.5 Quality Audit: IT Product Line

889. How does your organization know that its staff support services planning and management systems are appropriately effective and constructive?

890. How does your organization know whether they are adhering to mission and achieving objectives?

891. Has a written procedure been established to identify devices during all stages of receipt, reconditioning, distribution and installation so that mix-ups are prevented?

892. Are storage areas and reconditioning operations designed to prevent mix-ups and assure orderly handling of both the distressed and reconditioned devices?

893. How are you auditing your organizations compliance with regulations?

894. How does your organization know that its research planning and management systems are appropriately effective and constructive in enabling quality research outcomes?

895. Are there appropriate indicators for monitoring the effectiveness and efficiency of processes?

896. How does your organization know that its staff entrance standards are appropriately effective and constructive and being implemented consistently?

897. Do the suppliers use a formal quality system?

898. How does your organization know that its risk management system is appropriately effective and constructive?

899. How does your organization know that its public relations and marketing systems are appropriately effective and constructive?

900. How do you know what, specifically, is required of you in your work?

901. How does your organization know that its research programs are appropriately effective and constructive?

902. How does your organization know that the research supervision provided to its staff is appropriately effective and constructive?

903. How does your organization know that its quality of teaching is appropriately effective and constructive?

904. How does your organization know that the support for its staff is appropriately effective and constructive?

905. How does your organization know that its teaching activities (and staff learning) are effectively and constructively enhanced by its activities?

906. Is there any content that may be legally actionable?

907. How does your organization know that its system for inducting new staff to maximize workplace contributions are appropriately effective and constructive?

908. How does your organization know that its planning processes are appropriately effective and constructive?

3.6 Team Directory: IT Product Line

909. Process decisions: which organizational elements and which individuals will be assigned management functions?

910. What needs to be communicated?

911. What are you going to deliver or accomplish?

912. Who are the Team Members?

913. When does information need to be distributed?

914. Process decisions: are contractors adequately prosecuting the work?

915. Who will talk to the customer?

916. How and in what format should information be presented?

917. Decisions: is the most suitable form of contract being used?

918. Do purchase specifications and configurations match requirements?

919. Days from the time the issue is identified?

920. How do unidentified risks impact the outcome of the IT Product Line project?

921. How will you accomplish and manage the

objectives?

922. Does a IT Product Line project team directory list all resources assigned to the IT Product Line project?

923. Is construction on schedule?

924. Contract requirements complied with?

925. Who should receive information (all stakeholders)?

926. Decisions: what could be done better to improve the quality of the constructed product?

3.7 Team Operating Agreement: IT Product Line

927. Resource allocation: how will individual team members account for time and expenses, and how will this be allocated in the team budget?

928. Must your team members rely on the expertise of other members to complete tasks?

929. What are the boundaries (organizational or geographic) within which you operate?

930. Are there more than two native languages represented by your team?

931. Do you ensure that all participants know how to use the required technology?

932. What are the safety issues/risks that need to be addressed and/or that the team needs to consider?

933. What is a Virtual Team?

934. What is the anticipated procedure (recruitment, solicitation of volunteers, or assignment) for selecting team members?

935. Do you post meeting notes and the recording (if used) and notify participants?

936. Did you recap the meeting purpose, time, and expectations?

937. Did you draft the meeting agenda?

938. Are there more than two national cultures represented by your team?

939. Must your members collaborate successfully to complete IT Product Line projects?

940. How will your group handle planned absences?

941. Are team roles clearly defined and accepted?

942. Do you call or email participants to ensure understanding, follow-through and commitment to the meeting outcomes?

943. Are there the right people on your team?

944. Do you vary your voice pace, tone and pitch to engage participants and gain involvement?

945. Do you upload presentation materials in advance and test the technology?

946. The method to be used in the decision making process; Will it be consensus, majority rule, or the supervisor having the final say?

3.8 Team Performance Assessment: IT Product Line

947. To what degree do team members articulate the teams work approach?

948. To what degree will the team ensure that all members equitably share the work essential to the success of the team?

949. To what degree are the goals realistic?

950. To what degree will new and supplemental skills be introduced as the need is recognized?

951. What structural changes have you made or are you preparing to make?

952. To what degree do members articulate the goals beyond the team membership?

953. To what degree do team members understand one anothers roles and skills?

954. To what degree are corresponding categories of skills either actually or potentially represented across the membership?

955. Effects of crew composition on crew performance: Does the whole equal the sum of its parts?

956. To what degree are the skill areas critical to team

performance present?

957. When does the medium matter?

958. To what degree can all members engage in open and interactive considerations?

959. Do friends perform better than acquaintances?

960. To what degree does the teams purpose contain themes that are particularly meaningful and memorable?

961. To what degree do all members feel responsible for all agreed-upon measures?

962. To what degree can team members meet frequently enough to accomplish the teams ends?

963. To what degree are the relative importance and priority of the goals clear to all team members?

964. To what degree is there a sense that only the team can succeed?

965. How do you recognize and praise members for contributions?

966. How hard do you try to make a good selection?

3.9 Team Member Performance Assessment: IT Product Line

967. To what degree is the team cognizant of small wins to be celebrated along the way?

968. How do you use data to inform instruction and improve staff achievement?

969. To what degree are sub-teams possible or necessary?

970. How should adaptive assessments be implemented?

971. Can your organization rate by exception and assume that most employees are performing at an acceptable level?

972. Who they are?

973. To what degree are the goals ambitious?

974. How accurately is your plan implemented?

975. How are performance measures and associated incentives developed?

976. What happens if a team member receives a Rating of Unsatisfactory?

977. Verify business objectives. Are they appropriate, and well-articulated?

978. How do you start collaborating?

979. How will they be formed?

980. What does collaboration look like?

981. To what degree can team members frequently and easily communicate with one another?

982. Are the goals SMART ?

983. Why were corresponding selected?

984. How do you create a self-sustaining capacity for a collaborative culture?

3.10 Issue Log: IT Product Line

985. What does the stakeholder need from the team?

986. Is the issue log kept in a safe place?

987. How were past initiatives successful?

988. Which team member will work with each stakeholder?

989. What is the impact on the risks?

990. What would have to change?

991. What are the typical contents?

992. Are stakeholder roles recognized by your organization?

993. Where do team members get information?

994. What is a change?

995. What is a Stakeholder?

996. How often do you engage with stakeholders?

997. Why multiple evaluators?

998. Who do you turn to if you have questions?

999. Which stakeholders are thought leaders, influences, or early adopters?

1000. What steps can you take for positive relationships?

4.0 Monitoring and Controlling Process Group: IT Product Line

1001. How is agile IT Product Line project management done?

1002. How well did you do?

1003. What is the timeline?

1004. How are you doing?

1005. Is progress on outcomes due to your program?

1006. Is the program making progress in helping to achieve the set results?

1007. What good practices or successful experiences or transferable examples have been identified?

1008. How do you monitor progress?

1009. Are there areas that need improvement?

1010. How will staff learn how to use the deliverables?

1011. What resources (both financial and non-financial) are available/needed?

1012. What departments are involved in its daily operation?

1013. Does the solution fit in with organizations

technical architectural requirements?

1014. How is agile program management done?

4.1 Project Performance Report: IT Product Line

1015. To what degree are the demands of the task compatible with and converge with the mission and functions of the formal organization?

1016. What is in it for you?

1017. To what degree does the information network communicate information relevant to the task?

1018. To what degree does the task meet individual needs?

1019. To what degree do the structures of the formal organization motivate taskrelevant behavior and facilitate task completion?

1020. To what degree will the team adopt a concrete, clearly understood, and agreed-upon approach that will result in achievement of the teams goals?

1021. What is the degree to which rules govern information exchange between individuals within your organization?

1022. To what degree is the information network consistent with the structure of the formal organization?

1023. To what degree do the goals specify concrete team work products?

1024. To what degree does the formal organization make use of individual resources and meet individual needs?

1025. To what degree will the approach capitalize on and enhance the skills of all team members in a manner that takes into consideration other demands on members of the team?

1026. To what degree do team members frequently explore the teams purpose and its implications?

1027. To what degree does the teams work approach provide opportunity for members to engage in open interaction?

1028. To what degree do team members agree with the goals, relative importance, and the ways in which achievement will be measured?

4.2 Variance Analysis: IT Product Line

1029. At what point should variances be isolated and brought to the attention of the management?

1030. Do the rates and prices remain constant throughout the year?

1031. Are indirect costs accumulated for comparison with the corresponding budgets?

1032. What are the direct labor dollars and/or hours?

1033. Did a new competitor enter the market?

1034. Why are standard cost systems used?

1035. Wbs elements contractually specified for reporting of status to your organization (lowest level only)?

1036. Are there quarterly budgets with quarterly performance comparisons?

1037. Are there externalities from having some customers, even if they are unprofitable in the short run?

1038. Does the contractors system provide unit or lot costs when applicable?

1039. Is data disseminated to the contractors management timely, accurate, and usable?

1040. Are the overhead pools formally and adequately identified?

1041. Does the scheduling system identify in a timely manner the status of work?

1042. Who are responsible for the establishment of budgets and assignment of resources for overhead performance?

1043. How are variances affected by multiple material and labor categories?

1044. Are the actual costs used for variance analysis reconcilable with data from the accounting system?

1045. Who are responsible for overhead performance control of related costs?

1046. What is the performance to date and material commitment?

4.3 Earned Value Status: IT Product Line

1047. Are you hitting your IT Product Line projects targets?

1048. Validation is a process of ensuring that the developed system will actually achieve the stakeholders desired outcomes; Are you building the right product? What do you validate?

1049. Where is evidence-based earned value in your organization reported?

1050. Where are your problem areas?

1051. What is the unit of forecast value?

1052. When is it going to finish?

1053. How much is it going to cost by the finish?

1054. How does this compare with other IT Product Line projects?

1055. If earned value management (EVM) is so good in determining the true status of a IT Product Line project and IT Product Line project its completion, why is it that hardly any one uses it in information systems related IT Product Line projects?

1056. Verification is a process of ensuring that the developed system satisfies the stakeholders agreements and specifications; Are you building the product right? What do you verify?

1057. Earned value can be used in almost any IT Product Line project situation and in almost any IT Product Line project environment. it may be used on large IT Product Line projects, medium sized IT Product Line projects, tiny IT Product Line projects (in cut-down form), complex and simple IT Product Line projects and in any market sector. some people, of course, know all about earned value, they have used it for years - but perhaps not as effectively as they could have?

4.4 Risk Audit: IT Product Line

1058. Is IT Product Line project scope stable?

1059. Will safety checks of personal equipment supplied by competitors be conducted?

1060. Who is responsible for what?

1061. Is the customer willing to participate in reviews?

1062. Is there (or should there be) some impact on the process of setting materiality when the auditor more effectively identifies higher risk areas of the financial statements?

1063. What are the differences and similarities between strategic and operational risks in your organization?

1064. How do you govern assets?

1065. Is there a screening process that will ensure all participants have the fitness and skills required to safely participate?

1066. Will an appropriate standard of care be applied to all involved?

1067. Have all involved been advised of any obligations they have to sponsors?

1068. Have you considered the health and safety of everyone in your organization and do you meet work health and safety regulations?

1069. To what extent are auditors influenced by the business risk assessment in the audit process, and how can auditors create more effective mental models to more fully examine contradictory evidence?

1070. Does your organization have an up-to-date constitution?

1071. From an empirical perspective, does the business risk approach lead to a more effective audit, or simply to increased consulting revenue detrimental to audit rigor?

1072. Does your organization meet the terms of any contracts with which it is involved?

1073. Can analytical tests provide evidence that is as strong as evidence from traditional substantive tests?

1074. Assessing risk with analytical procedures: do systemsthinking tools help auditors focus on diagnostic patterns?

1075. What are the strategic implications with clients when auditors focus audit resources based on business-level risks?

1076. Has an event time line been developed?

1077. Is safety information provided to all involved?

4.5 Contractor Status Report: IT Product Line

1078. Describe how often regular updates are made to the proposed solution. Are corresponding regular updates included in the standard maintenance plan?

1079. What was the final actual cost?

1080. Are there contractual transfer concerns?

1081. What are the minimum and optimal bandwidth requirements for the proposed solution?

1082. What is the average response time for answering a support call?

1083. If applicable; describe your standard schedule for new software version releases. Are new software version releases included in the standard maintenance plan?

1084. What was the budget or estimated cost for your organizations services?

1085. Who can list a IT Product Line project as organization experience, your organization or a previous employee of your organization?

1086. How long have you been using the services?

1087. How does the proposed individual meet each requirement?

1088. What process manages the contracts?

1089. How is risk transferred?

1090. What was the actual budget or estimated cost for your organizations services?

1091. What was the overall budget or estimated cost?

4.6 Formal Acceptance: IT Product Line

1092. Do you buy-in installation services?

1093. Was the IT Product Line project work done on time, within budget, and according to specification?

1094. What can you do better next time?

1095. What is the Acceptance Management Process?

1096. Was the sponsor/customer satisfied?

1097. Who supplies data?

1098. Have all comments been addressed?

1099. What was done right?

1100. Was the IT Product Line project goal achieved?

1101. Did the IT Product Line project achieve its MOV?

1102. How well did the team follow the methodology?

1103. Was the client satisfied with the IT Product Line project results?

1104. Does it do what IT Product Line project team said it would?

1105. What function(s) does it fill or meet?

1106. Was business value realized?

1107. What lessons were learned about your IT Product Line project management methodology?

1108. How does your team plan to obtain formal acceptance on your IT Product Line project?

1109. Did the IT Product Line project manager and team act in a professional and ethical manner?

1110. Who would use it?

1111. What features, practices, and processes proved to be strengths or weaknesses?

5.0 Closing Process Group: IT Product Line

1112. How well defined and documented were the IT Product Line project management processes you chose to use?

1113. What will you do to minimize the impact should a risk event occur?

1114. What were the desired outcomes?

1115. What is the risk of failure to your organization?

1116. When will the IT Product Line project be done?

1117. Is the IT Product Line project funded?

1118. What can you do better next time, and what specific actions can you take to improve?

1119. Just how important is your work to the overall success of the IT Product Line project?

1120. Is this a follow-on to a previous IT Product Line project?

1121. How well did the chosen processes fit the needs of the IT Product Line project?

1122. How critical is the IT Product Line project success to the success of your organization?

1123. Is this an updated IT Product Line project Proposal Document?

1124. What were things that you did very well and want to do the same again on the next IT Product Line project?

1125. What areas were overlooked on this IT Product Line project?

1126. How dependent is the IT Product Line project on other IT Product Line projects or work efforts?

1127. What is the IT Product Line project Management Process?

1128. What do you need to do?

1129. Did the delivered product meet the specified requirements and goals of the IT Product Line project?

5.1 Procurement Audit: IT Product Line

1130. Does an appropriately qualified official check the quality of performance against the contract terms?

1131. Which are necessary components of a financial audit report under the Single Audit Act?

1132. Who is verifying the performance of the contract and approving payments?

1133. Is data securely stored?

1134. Is the procurement IT Product Line project efficiently managed?

1135. Does the strategy contain incentives to evaluate the performance of the procurement function/unit?

1136. Are approval limits covered in written procedures?

1137. Are the users needs clearly and invariably defined and has the expected outcome or mission been clearly identified and communicated in measurable terms?

1138. Has your organization taken a well-grounded decision about the procurement procedure chosen and has it documented the process?

1139. Is each copy of the purchase order necessary?

1140. Is a log maintained over the use of signature plates?

1141. Has an upper limit of cost been fixed?

1142. Did the conditions included in the contract protect the risk of non-performance by the supplier and were there no conflicting provisions?

1143. Are procurement processes well organized and documented?

1144. Were bids properly evaluated?

1145. Were additional deliveries a partial replacement for normal supplies or installations or an extension of existing supplies or installations?

1146. Is there no evidence of favouritism towards a particular contractor during the evaluation and negotiation processes?

1147. Are risks managed to provide reasonable assurance regarding department procurement objectives?

1148. Are there procedures to ensure that changes to purchase orders will be updated on the computer files?

1149. Is there a legal authority for the procurement IT Product Line project?

5.2 Contract Close-Out: IT Product Line

1150. Parties: who is involved?

1151. Have all acceptance criteria been met prior to final payment to contractors?

1152. How is the contracting office notified of the automatic contract close-out?

1153. Change in knowledge?

1154. Has each contract been audited to verify acceptance and delivery?

1155. Are the signers the authorized officials?

1156. How does it work?

1157. Have all contracts been closed?

1158. Change in attitude or behavior?

1159. What happens to the recipient of services?

1160. What is capture management?

1161. Have all contract records been included in the IT Product Line project archives?

1162. Was the contract sufficiently clear so as not to result in numerous disputes and misunderstandings?

1163. Have all contracts been completed?

1164. Why Outsource?

1165. Was the contract type appropriate?

1166. Was the contract complete without requiring numerous changes and revisions?

1167. Change in circumstances?

1168. How/when used ?

1169. Parties: Authorized?

5.3 Project or Phase Close-Out: IT Product Line

1170. If you were the IT Product Line project sponsor, how would you determine which IT Product Line project team(s) and/or individuals deserve recognition?

1171. What advantages do the an individual interview have over a group meeting, and vice-versa?

1172. Did the IT Product Line project management methodology work?

1173. Is there a clear cause and effect between the activity and the lesson learned?

1174. What is a Risk?

1175. What information did each stakeholder need to contribute to the IT Product Line projects success?

1176. What was learned?

1177. What security considerations needed to be addressed during the procurement life cycle?

1178. Which changes might a stakeholder be required to make as a result of the IT Product Line project?

1179. What is a Risk Management Process?

1180. What were the goals and objectives of the

communications strategy for the IT Product Line project?

1181. Who exerted influence that has positively affected or negatively impacted the IT Product Line project?

1182. Can the lesson learned be replicated?

1183. Were the outcomes different from the already stated planned?

1184. Have business partners been involved extensively, and what data was required for them?

1185. What were the actual outcomes?

1186. Were messages directly related to the release strategy or phases of the IT Product Line project?

1187. What was the preferred delivery mechanism?

5.4 Lessons Learned: IT Product Line

1188. What rewards do the individuals seek?

1189. What solutions or recommendations can you offer that would have improved some aspect of the IT Product Line project?

1190. What regulatory regime controlled how your organization head and program manager directed your organization and IT Product Line project?

1191. Did the team work well together?

1192. How effectively and timely was your organizational change impact identified and planned for?

1193. How many interest groups are stakeholders?

1194. Were any strategies or activities unsuccessful?

1195. What is below the surface?

1196. What was helpful to know when planning the deployment?

1197. How timely was the training you received in preparation for the use of the product/service?

1198. Who needs to learn lessons?

1199. How objective was the collection of data?

1200. Who has execution authority?

1201. How spontaneous are the communications?

1202. What is the distribution of authority?

1203. Will the information remain current?

1204. How to write up the lesson identified – how will you document the results of your analysis corresponding that you have an li ready to take the next step in the ll process?

1205. How effective was the quality assurance process?

Index

ability   34, 88
abnormal   181
absences   227
accept   208
acceptable   54, 79, 103, 230
acceptance   6, 120, 138, 140, 189, 220, 246-247, 252
accepted   118, 134, 169, 178, 227
accepting   136
access 2, 9-10, 60, 178
accomplish   7, 83, 106-107, 156, 180, 224, 229
according   30, 38, 196, 246
account   11, 31, 56, 151, 166, 226
accounting   150, 239
accounts   150
accuracy   171
accurate   10, 139, 152, 156, 238
accurately   124, 230
achievable   118
achieve   7, 69, 79, 83, 107, 156, 183, 190, 193, 201, 234, 240, 246
achieved   24, 81, 85, 124, 246
achieving   132, 221
acquire   214
acquired   154, 183
across 50, 228
action 49, 58, 93, 100, 102, 124, 131, 183, 195-196, 203
actionable   48, 107, 222
actions 19, 48, 95, 103, 106, 129, 195, 248
active 132, 135
actively   191
activities   20, 22, 26, 43, 87, 96, 101, 131-132, 154-156, 159-160, 167, 169, 172-173, 188, 195, 222, 256
activity 3-4, 31, 36, 153-162, 165, 168, 173-174, 254
actual 31, 55, 149-150, 173, 185, 239, 244-245, 255
actually   30, 65, 86, 102, 180, 182, 228, 240
adaptive   230
addition   8
additional   41, 61-62, 64, 70, 175, 197, 212, 251
additions   95
address   77, 129, 170, 203

making   21, 63, 78, 80, 87, 120, 183-184, 227, 234
manage   33, 38-39, 52-54, 68, 72, 78, 80, 82, 87, 90, 113,
125-126, 129, 133, 141, 169, 171, 192, 196, 207, 224
manageable 35, 85
managed   7, 41, 63, 71, 77, 82, 84, 97, 203, 250-251
management 1, 3-5, 9, 11-12, 21, 25, 40-41, 52, 61-63, 65, 72, 74,
77, 79-80, 83, 85, 91, 109, 111, 113, 116, 124, 133-137, 144-146,
150, 152-153, 156, 165-167, 169, 171-173, 177-180, 184-187, 189,
191, 193-195, 197, 203, 207, 209-210, 213-214, 220-222, 224, 234-
235, 238, 240, 246-249, 252, 254
manager   7, 12, 20, 33, 36, 106, 136, 144, 165, 207, 213, 247,
256
managers   2, 123, 149, 197-198, 203
manages   83, 88, 126, 245
managing   2, 84, 123, 128, 207
mandatory   217
manner   24, 90, 124, 185-186, 237, 239, 247
mapping   64, 66, 71, 211
market 26, 126, 158, 193, 238, 241
marketable   193
marketer   7
marketing   145, 222
markets   22
material   126, 150, 239
materials   1, 135, 227
matrices   141
Matrix 3-4, 129, 141, 185-186, 199, 212
matter 31, 52, 54, 229
matters   219
maximize   223
maximizing   113, 165
meaning   156
meaningful   57, 108, 229
measurable   34-35, 211, 250
measure   2, 12, 19, 21, 37, 39, 45, 47, 49-50, 52-54, 56, 65-
66, 76, 79-81, 85, 89, 93-94, 101, 131, 175-176, 181-183
measured   19, 46, 51, 56-57, 59, 82, 93-94, 182, 202, 237
measures   48, 50, 52-53, 57, 61-63, 66, 73, 84, 94, 100-101,
132, 183, 216, 229-230
measuring   96, 150
mechanical   1
mechanism   146, 215, 255
mechanisms   131, 135

provisions   251
public 222
publisher   1
purchase   9, 11, 224, 251
purchased   11
purpose   2, 11, 111, 126, 143, 175, 183, 220, 226, 229, 237
purposes   134, 171
pushing   117
qualified   30, 61, 66, 73, 133, 144, 250
qualifies   60, 66
qualify 48, 61
qualifying   169
qualities   27
quality 1, 4-5, 11, 21, 49-50, 53, 62, 64, 68, 73, 77, 94, 100, 124,
131, 143-144, 152, 169, 171-172, 174, 179, 181, 183-184, 187-190,
221-222, 225, 250, 257
quantified   102
quantify   48
quarterly   238
question   12-13, 17, 29, 45, 60, 76, 92, 105, 111, 132, 183
questions   7, 9, 12, 69, 168, 232
quickly 12, 69, 71-72, 194
radically   74
raised 143
rather 46, 114
Rating 230
rational   185
rationale   171
reached   26
reactivate   111
readiness   43, 204
readings   103
realistic   26, 63, 112, 199, 228
realize 50
realized   247
really   7, 20, 31, 186
reason 116, 209
reasonable   85, 111, 135, 174, 203, 207-208, 251
reasons   40, 189
reassigned   177
recast 173
recasts 174
receipt 221

result   70, 77, 82, 144, 173, 175, 177, 180-181, 218, 236, 252, 254
resulted   103
resulting   64
results 9, 31, 41, 54, 64, 76, 78-80, 82-84, 87, 91, 96, 100, 131-132,
136, 156, 173-174, 176, 179-180, 183, 185, 211, 234, 246, 257
retain   105, 179
retained   65
retention   53
return 77, 160
returns 181
revenue   24, 46, 243
revenues   56
review 11-12, 43, 55, 61, 160, 169, 172, 208, 220
reviewed   37, 152, 165, 169, 182, 207
reviews11, 145, 152, 185, 198, 203, 242
revised 72, 103, 201
revisions   253
revisit 219
reward 49, 54, 213
rewarded   25
rewards   95, 256
rework 48
rights   1
routine 97
safely 201, 242
safety 109, 226, 242-243
satisfied   173, 246
satisfies 240
satisfy 125
savings 43, 50, 57, 72
scalable   87
scenario   40, 43, 166
schedule   3-4, 38, 49, 99, 116, 132, 135, 149, 152-153, 161,
165, 169-170, 172, 185, 193, 203-204, 212, 217, 225, 244
scheduled   136-137, 189
schedules   161, 170
scheduling   152-153, 239
scheme   98
Scorecard   2, 13-15, 212
scorecards   95
Scores 15
scoring 11
screening   242